بِسْمِ اللهِ الرَّحْمٰنِ الرَّحِيْمِ

In the name of Allah—
The Most Merciful, The Most Kind

As the crescent moon appears and our honored guest, Ramadan, enters our homes, I extend my congratulations on reaching this blessed month. It is not by chance that you have made it to witness another Ramadan. *It is solely by Allah's (SWT) mercy.* He has granted you another opportunity to redeem yourself and gain the immense rewards of this beautiful month. *Ramadan Mubarak,* my sister. May this month bring you closer to Allah (SWT), and may it give you the strength and peace that your soul seeks. May your fasts be accepted, and your *dua'* answered. May your days be filled with light and love, and your nights enveloped in worship and forgiveness. May you find the strength to overcome your personal struggles, the wisdom to optimize on each day, and the happiness of sharing these moments with your family and loved ones. *Ameen.*

THE
Muslim Woman's
RAMADAN JOURNAL

*A 30-Day Planner for Reflection,
Inspiration & Spiritual Focus in the
Blessed Month of Ramadan*

by
KASHMIR MARYAM

mindful
MUSLIM
PRESS

kashmirmaryam.com
mindfulmuslimpress.org

Copyright © 2025 Kashmir Maryam
A publication of Mindful Muslim Press

Cover Design by Muhammad Z.
Illustrations by Aleena Masroor
Interior Design by Ravi Ramgati

Paperback ISBN 979-8-9917013-2-7
Hardcover ISBN 979-8-9917013-3-4

other works by
KASHMIR MARYAM

The Muslim Woman's Manifesto
10 Steps to Achieving Phenomenal Success,
in Both Worlds

The Muslim Woman's Journal
A Book of Reflective Writing Prompts to Inspire
a Successful Mindset, a Life Brimming with
Purpose & a Deeper Connection to Allah

Be Soft, Be Strong
Inspirational Reminders for Muslim Women

Nafsi
Jihad Upon My Self

My Quran Journal
A Daily Companion for Reflecting
on the Words of Allah

CONTENTS

01
ESSENTIAL DUA'
A Useful List of Dua' to Recite Daily
During Ramadan
(page 25)

02
MY PERSONAL DUA' LIST
A Special Place to Write Your Dua'
During This Blessed Month
(page 43)

03
99 NAMES OF ALLAH (SWT)
A space to connect & reflect on the
beautiful names & attributes
of Allah (SWT)
(page 49)

04
MY QURAN READING LOG
A Space to Track Your Daily Recitation Goals &
to Ponder Upon the Meanings of The Quran
(page 59)

05
MY HABIT TRACKER
Think About the Habits You Want to Build &
Those you Want to Leave Behind
(page 81)

Introduction

*"Whoever observes fasting during the month of Ramadan
out of sincere faith and hoping to attain Allah's rewards
then all his past sins will be forgiven."*

—The Prophet Muhammad (SAW)
[Bukhari 38]

I'm not sure about you, but after every Ramadan, I find myself thinking, "*I wish I could have done more. I wish I had planned better—structured my days more intentionally. I wish I had balanced my time between worship, family and work better.*" The list goes on, and each year feels more overwhelming than the last.

This year, I knew I wanted Ramadan to be different. I wanted to welcome it wholeheartedly like the beloved guest it is. I wanted to devote the level of attention to it that it truly deserves. I also wanted to accept what is realistic given all of my responsibilities without punishing myself for the things outside of my control. I realized that the only way to achieve this would be to *plan* better. That meant spiritually, mentally *and* physically.

Reflecting over the example of the *sahaaba*, it was confirmed to me that the key *must* be in preparation. The companions of the Prophet (SAW), would start preparing for Ramadan six months in advance. As Ibn Rajab al-Hanbali noted, *"They (the Salaf) used to ask Allah to allow them to reach Ramadan six months in advance, and then they would pray for another six months that Allah accept their efforts in Ramadan."* Their devotion, preparation and foresight was a powerful reminder to me about the importance of approaching this sacred month with intention and preparation. But the question is *Why*? Why were they so diligent in this? It was because they understood the status of Ramadan. They understood the unique blessings and opportunities that elevate Ramadan above all other months of the year. They understood that Ramadan was a priceless opportunity to draw closer to

Allah (SWT). They seized every moment, knowing that letting this sacred month slip by without fully embracing its rewards would be an undeniable loss. This understanding fueled the pious predecessors to carefully plan and map out how they would spend their time in this sacred month. Reflecting on their dedication, I realized I needed to shift my mindset. I want to be among the forerunners—those who strive with passion for Allah's (SWT) pleasure. After all, our striving for Him is directly proportional to how much we truly want *Jannah*—a place we all long and pray to enter one day.

And that's how *The Muslim Woman's Ramadan Journal* was born. It is primarily something I created for myself—a place to gather my thoughts, log my recitation of the Quran, and to draft a careful plan for how I wanted my Ramadan to look. I realized that other Muslim sisters might benefit from the structure and focus this journal offers. With that in mind, I turned it into a manuscript, ensuring it was comprehensive and tailored to our unique journey as women, while also keeping it easy to follow and practical for everyday use.

This journal is about grounding your intentions in purpose and translating that intention into meaningful actions. By doing so, you will embody your *eman* in ways that, *Insha'Allah*, will earn Allah's (SWT) pleasure. May He accept your efforts and bless you on this journey. *Ameen.*

This journal also offers a space for you to balance your many roles while seeking spiritual and emotional fulfillment during Ramadan. It is a place where you can center yourself when feeling thirsty, hungry, or energy-depleted. For this reason, you'll notice a great deal of focus on mindfulness in this journal. As a therapist, I *had* to include this. This is because mindfulness is a deeply spiritual process. It clears your mind and facilitates *khushoo'*. This clarity then paves the way for you to reflect on the verses of Allah (SWT) and the teachings of our Prophet Muhammad (SAW). When your minds is clearer, your spirituality grows. *Everything is connected.*

Fasting purifies our souls, cleanses our bodies, and brings clarity to our minds. This journal supports that process by focusing on all three: mind, body, and soul. If you want to make meaningful spiritual progress, you must nurture each of these aspects, as they are all deeply interconnected. Whether you are managing a household, working, caring for family, studying, or juggling multiple roles, this journal is here to help you integrate all of these elements and make the most of Ramadan.

The Beautiful Virtues of Ramadan

As we mentioned earlier, it is not enough to simply create a plan. The real key to sustainable action and willpower lies in understanding the motivation behind that plan—your "why." This is something the earliest generations of Muslims understood deeply. They recognized the immense value of planning for Ramadan because they truly grasped its virtues. So, let's explore that a bit further. Understanding why this month is so special will give you the drive to make the most of it.

Why Do We Fast as Muslims?

On the surface, Ramadan is understood as a month of fasting from food and drink from dawn until dusk. While this is correct, fasting is much more than simply abstaining from these physical needs. The Messenger of Allah (SAW) taught us:

"Whoever does not give up false statements (i.e. telling lies), and evil deeds, and speaking bad words to others, Allah is not in need of his (fasting) leaving his food and drink."

—The Prophet Muhammad (SAW)
[Bukhari 6057]

From this, we understand that simply refraining from food and drink is not the full definition of fasting. Fasting is about attaining *taqwa* (piety) and submitting to Allah (SWT). *Taqwa* encompasses both fulfilling the commands of Allah (SWT) and abstaining from what He has prohibited. Allah (SWT) Himself tells us this in the Quran:

"Oh you who believe! Observing the fasting is prescribed for you as it was prescribed for those before you, that you may become pious."

—The Quran (2:183)

This verse highlights the deeper purpose of fasting: gaining righteousness and piety through obedience to Allah (SWT). In fact, a notable characteristic of a sincere believer is in their hastening to obey the commands of Allah (SWT) and His messenger (SAW). We know this because of what Allah (SWT) says in Surah Noor:

"The only saying of the faithful believers, when they are called to Allah (His Words, the Quran) and His Messenger, to judge between them, is that they say: 'We hear and we obey.' And such are the successful (who will live forever in Paradise)."

—The Quran (24:51)

This means that we fast because we are obeying Allah's (SWT) command, first and foremost. While the physical act of fasting may seem straightforward, Allah (SWT) has hidden many benefits in it that we might not fully grasp. As He tells us in the Quran:

"... and fasting is better for you, if only you knew."

—The Quran (2:184)

This tells us that regardless of the physical or spiritual benefits fasting may offer, we do not fast *because* of them. Rather, we fast simply because Allah (SWT) has commanded us to. *We hear, and we obey.* As a side note, we accept that there are other virtues— whether we are aware of them or not.

Now that we have established that the primary reason we fast in Ramadan is because Allah (SWT) commanded us to, we can explore the special features unique to Ramadan.

A Month of Forgiveness

One of the most profound gifts of Ramadan is the chance for spiritual renewal and forgiveness. As the Prophet Muhammad (SAW) beautifully informed us:

"When Ramadan begins, the gates of Heaven are opened, the gates of Hell are closed, and the devils are chained."

—The Prophet Muhammad (SAW)
[Bukhari 1899]

"Whoever observes fasting during the month of Ramadan out of sincere faith and hoping to attain Allah's rewards then all his past sins will be forgiven."

—The Prophet Muhammad (SAW)
[Bukhari 38]

Reflecting on these divinely inspired words of our Messenger (SAW) reminds us that completing the fast in the month of Ramadan leads to the forgiveness of all past sins. *This knowledge is a powerful motivator.* Knowing this should encourage us to create a sacred atmosphere in our homes and *masajid*, where we can focus on worship, nurture our relationship with Allah (SWT), and seek forgiveness for past mistakes. If there is ever a time to wipe the slate clean and start fresh, it is during Ramadan.

The Month of the Quran

The month of Ramadan holds a special place in Islam because it marks the revelation of the Glorious Quran. As Allah (SWT) says:

"The month of Ramadan is that in which was revealed the Quran, a guidance for the people and clear proofs of guidance and criterion."

—The Quran (2:185)

This verse indicates that the Quran's revelation began during Ramadan. Scholars explain that the Quran was first sent down from the *Lawhul Mahfuz* (the Preserved Tablet) to the lowest heaven, known as *Bayt ul-'Izzah* (the House of Honor), on *Laylat ul-Qadr,* a night in Ramadan. From there, it was revealed incrementally over 23 years to the Prophet Muhammad (SAW) by the Angel Jibreel (Gabriel).

This connection between Ramadan and The Quran emphasizes the importance of engaging with the Book of Allah (SWT) during this time. This means we must make a concerted effort to read and understand the meanings of the Quran *especially* during this special month.

Many Muslims around the world set a goal to complete reading the entire Quran during Ramadan. While there is abundant reward for each letter read, it is crucial that we do not become a nation of readers without implementing its teachings. In fact, it is more beloved to Allah (SWT) when we read, reflect, and act on what we read. This means that reading with *mindfulness* should take precedence over simply racing to finish. Remember, there is no finish line—your competition is your *Self.* Strive to be better than you were last year. So make it a goal to finish the Quran—but also make it a goal to take your time contemplating each verse and applying its teachings to your life.

It should also be noted that while it is *mustahabb* (recommended) for Muslims to read the Quran extensively during Ramadan and strive to complete it, it is not obligatory. In other words, if you do not finish reading the Quran, you are not sinning, though you will have missed out on a great deal of reward. The evidence for this is:

"Jibreel used to review the Quran with the Prophet (SAW) once every year, but he reviewed it with him twice in the year he passed away."

[Bukhari]

It was also noted that Aishah (RA), the wife of the Prophet Muhammad (SAW) was asked about his character, she responded:

"His character was the Quran."

[Muslim]

This statement indicates that the Prophet Muhammad (SAW) embodied the teachings and morals of the Quran in his daily actions. This description highlights how closely he followed the guidance of the Quran—not only reading it but manifesting it in his actions. What an excellent example we have been given in this beautiful religion of Islam, which prioritizes actions and intentions over mere knowledge and rote recitation.

Interestingly, Allah (SWT) also teaches us what to avoid in a well-known hadith. The Prophet Muhammad (SAW) warned about a group called the *Khawarij*, those who rebelled against the Muslim community, saying:

"There will appear a people among my Ummah who will recite the Quran, but it will not go past their throats. They will pass through Islam as an arrow passes through its target..."

—The Prophet Muhammad (SAW)
[Ibn Majah 170]

The reference to the Quran not going beyond their throats implies that, although they may recite it fluently or even frequently, the words do not reach their hearts or influence their actions with genuine faith. Instead, their focus on outward recitation is not accompanied by sincere understanding or humility. This metaphor cautions against superficial religiosity and emphasizes the importance of true belief and internalizing the Quran's message.

It should also be mentioned here that oftentimes non-Muslims wonder in amazement how we can fast for 30 days—without food and water. Yet somehow Allah (SWT) makes it easier for us the more we do it. We are capable of great feats when we devote the time and energy to it, backed up by the power of faith. In the same way, we are capable of reading and reflecting more intensively from the Quran when we truly apply ourselves. So this year, *I want you to challenge yourself.* I want you to push yourself to new limits. But this can only happen if you set your intentions clearly and plan ahead. *Plan. Plan. Plan.*

Since the power of planning can greatly aid you in this journey, I encourage you to make the most of the Quran Reading Log in this journal. It will help you track your progress toward completing your personal reading and reflection goals each day. Additionally, the Daily Planner includes a section to monitor both your recitation and reflection goals.

Ramadan—Your *Golden* Ticket

The virtues of Ramadan are vast, and the potential rewards for good deeds during this month are exponential. It is undeniable that Ramadan presents an incredible opportunity to engage in acts of worship that can significantly impact the trajectory of your hereafter. One striking hadith that reinforces this, and has always resonated with me, is the story narrated by the companion Talha ibn 'Ubaydallah (RA). He shared a story of two men who embraced Islam together. One was martyred after participating in many battles, while the other passed away a year later. In a dream, Talha saw the second man entering Paradise before the martyr. Confused, he asked the Prophet Muhammad (SAW) about it. The Prophet (SAW) explained:

"Did he not remain behind him for one year? Did he not reach Ramadan, fast, and pray with such and such number of prostrations in the year? The difference between them is greater than what is between the heavens and the earth."

—The Prophet Muhammad (SAW)
[Ibn Majah 3925]

This powerful reminder highlights that the acts of devotion during Ramadan can elevate our status in ways that outward appearances or heroic deeds cannot. Each fast, each prayer, and each moment of sincerity matters in Allah's (SWT) eyes. This is a call to meet each Ramadan with gratitude and zeal.

It's not by chance that you're here. Allah (SWT) has gifted you this opportunity—make the most of it.

May Allah (SWT) give you the strength to fully experience Ramadan, accept your efforts, and pardon your shortcomings. May He protect you from evil and inspire you towards the light of faith. And may He grant you a place amongst the righteous in *Jannatul Firdaws. Ameen.*

How to Use
This Journal

"The soul is in need of two things: knowledge and action. Planning is a form of knowledge that leads to effective action."

—Ibn Qayyim al-Jawziyya

As you step into the beautiful journey of Ramadan, think of this journal as your loyal companion. Take it with you as you go about your day. Review it in the morning and reflect in it at night. It is here to encourage intention and reflection for every single day of Ramadan. To make it easier for you to visualize, you can find a breakdown of each section of this journal in the table below.

Chapter	*Description*
ESSENTIAL DUA'	Contains all the important *dua'* that you will need for closing and then opening your fast, as well as general *adhkhar* to recite throughout your day.
MY PERSONAL DUA' LIST	A special space for your personal prayers. Use this section to write down your requests and *dua'*. It is encouraged that you revisit these frequently throughout the month for spiritual focus—especially in the last ten nights of Ramadan.
MY QURAN READING LOG	Track your personalized Quran recitation goals here—perfect if you're trying to finish reading the entire Quran this Ramadan. This log also helps you to reflect over the meanings of the verses, deepening your connection to the Quran during this month.
99 NAMES OF ALLAH	A space to connect & reflect on the beautiful names & attributes of Allah (SWT).
MY HABIT TRACKER	Identify habits you want to overcome and brainstorm strategies for breaking free from them. This space is designed to help you recognize patterns that hinder your spiritual growth. It is also a space for you to cultivate positive habits by listing beneficial practices you wish to incorporate into your routine. Track your progress to stay motivated throughout Ramadan.
MY RAMADAN REFLECTIONS	Reflect on your personal experiences from last Ramadan. Jot down lessons learned and goals for this Ramadan.
RAMADAN REFRAME	Strategies for building a growth mindset about Ramadan. This will encourage positivity and resilience in your spiritual journey over the next 30 days.
PRODUCTIVITY HACKS	Enhance your time management skills with practical tips tailored for balancing worship and daily responsibilities during Ramadan.

Chapter	Description
THE SUNNAH FOOD GUIDE	Plan meals using this section. This chapter highlights nutritious foods from the *sunnah* that will enhance your physical health and energy.
A MAMA'S GUIDE	A creative guide for mothers on engaging children in Ramadan. This section includes family bonding activities that encourage children to get involved in understanding and observing this holy month.
NAVIGATING YOUR CYCLE	Practical tips for navigating your period during Ramadan so that you can still engage in spiritual growth whilst on your cycle.
SEEKING LAYLATUL QADR	A dedicated space for exploring the virtues of the last ten nights of Ramadan. This section includes spiritual & practical ways to prepare and observe The Night of Power.
EID UL-FITR	A guide to celebrating Eid— the *sunnah* way.
MY GIFT LIST	Create a list of thoughtful Eid gifts for your loved ones.
MY DAILY PLANNER	Create a structured daily plan that includes the following sections, and more: • *Salah* tracker • Daily Quran recitation tracker • Meal plan (*suhoor* and *iftar*) • My schedule (hour by hour) • Acts of *sadaqah* tracker • Physical fitness tracker • Mindfulness tracker (includes a mood tracker, self-care check-in, and a section designated for reflections on physical/ emotional/ spiritual state)
FAREWELL RAMADAN	An opportunity to cherish & reflect on lessons learned this Ramadan.

A *Mindful* Ramadan Journal

Ramadan is a beautiful month. It will challenge us to push our endurance physically, spiritually, *and* mentally. So it becomes crucial for us to prioritize ways in which we can support ourselves and our families if we want to be prepared to succeed and excel in this month.

Naturally, as a therapist, I believe that nurturing our minds is essential to nurturing our souls. It is for this reason that this Ramadan journal has been thoughtfully designed with a holistic approach in mind, recognizing that true purification during Ramadan encompasses the physical, the mental, and the spiritual.

"He who does not possess a sound mind cannot find rest, for the heart cannot be at peace without the mind being at ease."

—Ibn Al-Qayyim

Throughout this journal, you will find dedicated sections that focus specifically on mindfulness and mental health as we navigate this sacred time. These spaces encourage you to take a step back, breathe deeply, and reflect on your emotions throughout the month. It's easy to get caught up in the hustle and bustle of fasting, cooking, traveling to the masjid along with other family and work commitments. That is why I encourage you to carve out small moments for self-care. Whether it is a few minutes of quiet reflection, reading some *adkhaar*, or even journaling your thoughts; these practices can help you recharge and find balance—even on the busiest days.

You will also find prompts for mindfulness and emotional check-ins in the Daily Planner. Take these moments as pit stops to practice self-care and show kindness to yourself. Remember, every little effort counts, and prioritizing your mental well-being will only enhance your spiritual journey.

How to Use this Journal

*"The believer is like a bee; it eats what is pure, and
it produces what is pure, and it plans its actions with wisdom."*

—Ibn Abbas

I want you to see this journal as your wise companion throughout Ramadan. It is designed to introduce you to this month before it even begins. The introductory chapters will help you get a firm understanding of its virtues and opportunities for rewards; this will allow you to appreciate the avenues by which you can use to draw closer to Allah (SWT). So please take your time and read through the chapters in-depth to get a clear understanding of the ways in which Allah (SWT) wants us to observe this month.

The later sections of this journal are more interactive. Here you'll be able to meticulously plan out your days using the hour-by-hour schedules. You will also find dedicated spaces for *adh-kaar*, reading the Quran (no matter your commitment level), *salah*, family time, self-care, and more. It is recommended to complete your plan the night before. This allows you to organize your time precisely so you'll be able to focus on implementing your plan the next day.

While some might view this as "over-planning," for those eager to seize every opportunity for *hasanaat*, this approach is *invaluable*. I promise that with focus and commitment, you will never regret this effort. Remember: if you fail to plan, you only plan to fail.

With this in mind, this journal is designed to be compact in size, making it easy for you to carry in your purse, allowing you to stay focused and centered throughout your day. Bring it with you to work, to the *masjid* in the evenings, or complete it from the comfort and privacy of your own home as you please. It is highly recommended that you read and fill out your plan consistently, ideally every day. This consistency will help you achieve the best possible results.

I know life can get busy—but do not lose sight of what truly matters. Our days on this earth are numbered, but if we capitalize on the opportunities that Allah (SWT) has gifted us with, then we can strive to meet Him with content hearts—pleased with Him, and Him pleased with us.

You've got this, my sister.

Essential Dua'

A Useful List of Dua' to Recite Daily During Ramadan

"Nothing is more honorable before Allah than dua (supplication)."

—The Prophet Muhammad (SAW)
[Al-Hakim]

In Islam, *dua* (supplication) is the most intimate form of conversation with Allah (SWT). It allows us to communicate our deepest needs, desires, and gratitude in a way that is unique between a slave and their Creator. No other conversation comes close to this. The act of making *dua* is actually a form of worship and submission—an acknowledgment of Allah's (SWT) sovereignty. As the Prophet Muhammad (SAW) said, "*Dua is worship*" [Tirmidhi 3372].

The Power of Supplication in Ramadan

During Ramadan, the power of *dua* (supplication) is unparalleled. Allah (SWT) promises in the Quran, "*Call upon Me; I will respond to you.*" (40:60). This assurance reaches its peak during the last ten nights, especially *Laylatul Qadr*, a night of immense blessings and forgiveness.

The Prophet Muhammad (SAW) emphasized that Allah (SWT) is especially close during this time, ready to accept sincere *dua*'. To seize this opportunity, approach these nights with focus and consistency, striving to make each moment count.

Etiquettes for Effective Supplication

Allah (SWT) said:

> "*Your Lord has proclaimed, 'Call upon Me
> [i.e. believe in Islamic monotheism and ask Me
> for anything], I will respond to you...'*"

—The Quran (40:60)

From this verse, we learn that when we call upon Allah (SWT), we must do so with complete certainty that He hears every word, understands every need, and will respond in the way that is best for us.

Many Muslims may not realize that there's an "art" to making *dua*—a set of etiquettes that can enhance the likelihood of Allah (SWT) accepting it. These etiquettes help strengthen the sincerity and focus behind our supplications. Here are some key ones to keep in mind:

1. FIRM BELIEF IN TAWHEED

Our hearts should be filled with a deep conviction in the oneness of Allah (SWT)—His divinity, Lordship, and beautiful names and attributes. Allah (SWT) says:

"And when My slaves ask you (Oh Muhammad) concerning Me, then (answer them), I am indeed near (to them by My Knowledge). I respond to the invocations of the supplicant when he calls on Me (without any mediator or intercessor). So let them obey Me and believe in Me, so that they may be led aright."

—The Quran (2:186)

From this we can understand that *dua* is not just about asking—it is about *responding* to Allah (SWT) with obedience and trust.

2. SINCERITY IS KEY

Dua is a form of worship, so it should be made sincerely for Allah (SWT) alone. Allah (SWT) reminds us:

"And they were commanded not, but that they should worship Allah, and worship none but Him Alone (abstaining from ascribing partners to Him)."

—The Quran (98:5)

3. CALL UPON ALLAH (SWT) BY HIS BEAUTIFUL NAMES

When you make *dua*, use Allah's (SWT) names. For example, if seeking forgiveness, call upon Him as *Al-Ghaffar* (The Forgiving). Allah (SWT) says:

"And (all) the Most Beautiful Names belong to Allah, so call on Him by them, and leave the company of those who belie or deny (or utter impious speech against) His Names."

—The Quran (7:180)

4. BEGIN WITH PRAISE AND BLESSINGS

Start your *dua* by praising Allah (SWT) and sending blessings upon the Prophet (SAW). The Prophet Muhammad (SAW) taught us to first glorify Allah (SWT) and send *salawat* before presenting our requests. Fadalah Ibn 'Ubayd (RA) said:

"Whilst the Messenger of Allah (SAW) was sitting, a man came in and prayed and said, "Oh Allah, forgive me and have mercy on me."

The Messenger of Allah (SAW) said, "You have been too hasty, oh worshipper. When you have prayed and are sitting, praise Allah as He deserves to be praised, and send blessings upon me, then call upon Him."

[Tirmidhi 3476]

5. SEND SALAWAT (BLESSINGS) UPON THE PROPHET (SAW)

The Prophet (SAW) said:

"When one of you prays, let him start with praise of Allah, then let him send blessings upon the Prophet (SAW), then let him ask whatever he likes after that."

Then another man prayed after that, and he praised Allah and sent blessings upon the Prophet (SAW). The Prophet (SAW) said: 'Oh worshipper, ask and you will be answered.'"

—The Prophet Muhammad (SAW)
[Tirmidhi 3477]

6. FACE THE QIBLAH

Turning towards the *qiblah* is recommended when making *dua*. This was the practice of the Prophet (SAW) during moments of intense supplication, like before the Battle of *Badr*. Umar ibn al-Khattab (RA) said:

"On the day of Badr, the Messenger of Allah (SAW) looked at the mushrikeen (polytheists), who were one thousand strong, and his Companions numbered three hundred and nineteen. Then the Prophet of Allah (SAW) turned to face the qiblah, then he stretched forth his hands and started to cry out to his Lord:

"Oh Allah, grant me what You have promised me, Oh Allah, give me what You have promised me. Oh Allah, if this small band of Muslims perishes, You will not be worshipped on earth."

He kept on crying out to his Lord, stretching forth his hands, facing towards the qiblah, until his cloak fell from his shoulders..."

[Muslim 1763]

7. RAISE YOUR HANDS

Raise your hands in humility towards the heavens, as a beggar would—with the palms upward, and the hands held together (without any gap between them). The Prophet Muhammad (SAW) said:

"Your Lord, may He be blessed and exalted, is Kind and Most Generous, and He is too kind to let His slave, if he raises his hands to Him, bring them back empty."

—The Prophet Muhammad (SAW)
[Ibn Majah 3865]

8. HAVE CERTAINTY THAT ALLAH (SWT) WILL RESPOND

Make *dua* with a focused mind and heart, and have complete trust that Allah (SWT) will respond. The Prophet (SAW) said:

"Call upon Allah while you are certain of a response, and know that Allah does not answer a dua from a negligent and heedless heart."

—The Prophet Muhammad (SAW)
[Tirmidhi]

9. BE PERSISTENT–BUT NOT HASTY

Ask often and don't lose hope if you do not see an immediate response. The Prophet (SAW) said:

"The slave will receive a response so long as his dua does not involve sin or severing of family ties, and so long as he is not hasty." It was said, "What does being hasty mean?"
He said: "When he says, 'I made dua and I made dua, and I have not seen any response,' and he gets frustrated and stops making dua."

—The Prophet Muhammad (SAW)
[Bukhari]

10. BE FIRM WHEN ASKING ALLAH (SWT)

Ask Allah (SWT) with conviction. The Prophet (SAW) said:

"No one of you should say, 'Oh Allah, forgive me if You wish, Oh Allah, have mercy on me if You wish'; he should be firm in his asking, for Allah cannot be compelled."

—The Prophet Muhammad (SAW)
[Bukhari 6339]

11. APPROACH WITH HUMILITY, HOPE, AND FEAR

Dua should be a balance of love, hope in Allah's (SWT) mercy, and fear of His displeasure. Allah (SWT) says:

"Verily, they used to hasten to do good deeds, and they used to call on Us with hope and fear and used to humble themselves before Us."

—The Quran (21:90)

"Remember your Lord inwardly with humility and reverence and in a moderate tone of voice, both morning and evening."

—The Quran (7:205)

12. REPEAT YOUR DUA THREE TIMES

The Prophet (SAW) would often repeat his *dua* three times for emphasis and sincerity. Abdullah ibn Mas'ud (RA) said:

"Whilst the Messenger of Allah (SAW) was praying at the Ka'bah, Abu Jahl and his companions were sitting nearby. They had slaughtered a camel the previous day, and Abu Jahl said: "Which of you will go and get the abdominal contents of the camel of Banu so-and-so and put it on the back of Muhammad when he prostrates?" The worst of the people went and got it, and when the Prophet (SAW) prostrated, he placed it between his shoulders. They started laughing, leaning against one another. I was standing there watching, and if I had had any power, I would have lifted it from the back of the Messenger of Allah (SAW).

The Prophet (SAW) remained in prostration, not lifting his head, until someone went and told Fatimah. She came with Juwayriyah, and lifted it from him, then she turned to them and rebuked them.

When the Prophet (SAW) had finished his prayer, he raised his voice and prayed against them—and when he made dua or asked of Allah he would repeat it three times, and he said: "Oh Allah, punish Quraysh" three times.

When they heard his voice, they stopped laughing and were afraid because of his dua.

Then he said, "Oh Allah, punish Abu Jahl Ibn Hisham, Utbah Ibn Rabi'ah, Shaybah Ibn Rabi'ah, Al-Walidibn 'Uqbah, Umayyah Ibn Khalaf and Uqbah Ibn Abu Mu'ayt," and he mentioned the seventh but I cannot remember who it was. By the One Who sent Muhammad (SAW) with the truth, I saw those whom he had named slain on the day of Badr, then they were dragged and thrown into the well—the well of Badr."

[Bukhari 240]

13. CONSUME HALAL PROVISIONS

Ensure that your food, drink, and clothing are *halal*. The Prophet (SAW) warned that consuming haram acts as a barrier to having *dua* accepted. He (SAW) said:

"Oh people! Allah is Pure and, therefore, accepts only that which is pure. Allah has commanded the believers as He has commanded His Messengers by saying: 'Oh Messengers! Eat of the good things, and do good deeds.' (23:51) And He said: 'Oh you who believe (in the Oneness of Allah)! Eat of the lawful things that We have provided you...'" (2:172). Then he (SAW) made a mention of the person who travels for a long period of time, his hair is disheveled and covered with dust. He lifts his hand towards the sky and thus makes the supplication: 'My Rabb! My Rabb!' But his food is unlawful, his drink is unlawful, his clothes are unlawful and his nourishment is unlawful. How then can his supplication be accepted?"

—The Prophet Muhammad (SAW)
[Muslim]

14. MAKE DUA PRIVATELY

Say your *dua* in private, and in a humble and low voice. Allah (SWT) says:

> *"Invoke your Lord with humility and in secret."*
>
> —The Quran (7:55)

And Allah (SWT) praised the prophet Zakariyyah (RA) by saying:

> *"When he called to his Lord (Allah)—a call in secret."*
>
> —The Quran (19:3)

By observing these etiquettes, we can strive to approach *dua* in the best possible manner within our capacity. The outcome, as always, is left to Allah (SWT).

The Role of Patience in Supplication

One of the most profound aspects of supplication is the acknowledgment that the response may not always come as expected or in *our* desired timeframe. After all, as humans we were created in haste:

> *"Man was created of haste [i.e., impatience]…"*
>
> —The Quran (21:37)

However, the absence of an immediate answer does not mean it was rejected. Allah (SWT) may respond by granting us something better, protecting us from harm, or rewarding us in the Hereafter. The Prophet (SAW) said:

"No Muslim makes supplication—unless he is someone who has cut off his relatives—but that he is given one of three things: (1) either his supplication is answered quickly, or (2) it is stored up for him in the next world, or (3) an evil equal to it is averted from him."

—The Prophet Muhammad (SAW)
[Bukhari]

During Ramadan, we are especially reminded to trust in the timing and wisdom of Allah (SWT). Supplication itself becomes an ongoing act of submission, trust, and patience, reinforcing the understanding that Allah's (SWT) plan for us is far greater than anything we could imagine.

Making Supplication a Part of Everyday Life

While supplication holds special significance during Ramadan, it should not be limited to this sacred month. As Muslims, we are encouraged to make *dua* a daily practice, as consistently turning to Allah (SWT) strengthens our bond with Him.

To make the most of this section in the journal, consider using the following *dua* to guide you through Ramadan. Additionally, it is highly recommended to refer to comprehensive collections like *The Fortress of the Muslim* for a more specific range of supplications.

DUA TO REACH RAMADAN

When to say it: Before reaching Ramadan

اَللّٰهُمَّ سَلِّمْنِيْ إِلَى رَمَضَانَ وَسَلِّمْ لِي رَمَضَانَ وَتَسَلَّمْه مِنِّي مُتَقَبَّلا

*Allahumma sallimni ila Ramadan wa sallim
li Ramadan wa tasallamhu minni mutaqabbala*

Oh Allah! Preserve me until Ramadan, safeguard Ramadan
for me and accept it from me (receive my deeds
with acceptance).

DUA WHEN CLOSING FAST (SUHOOR)

When to say it: When closing your fast at *suhoor* time

وَبِصَوْمِ غَدٍ نَوَيْتُ مِنْ شَهْرِ رَمَضَانَ

Wa bisawmi ghadin nawaytu min shahri Ramadan

I intend to fast tomorrow for the month of Ramadan.

DUA AFTER BREAKING FAST (IFTAR)

When to Say It: After breaking your fast during
Ramadan or any other fast.

ذَهَبَ الظَّمَأُ، وَابْتَلَّتِ الْعُرُوقُ، وَثَبَتَ الْأَجْرُ إِنْ شَاءَ اللّٰهُ

*Dhahaba al-dhama' wabtalat al-'urooq wa thabata al-ajr
insha'Allah*

Gone is the thirst, the veins are moistened, and the reward is
confirmed, if Allah (SWT) wills.

DUA BEFORE EATING

بِسْمِ اللَّهِ وَعَلَى بَرَكَةِ اللَّهِ

bismillah wa 'ala barakatillah

In the name of Allah and upon the blessings of Allah.

DUA AFTER EATING

الْحَمْدُ لِلَّهِ الَّذِي أَطْعَمَنَا وَسَقَانَا وَجَعَلَنَا مُسْلِمِينَ

Alhamdulillah alladhi at'amana wa saqana wa ja'alana muslimeen

All praise is due to Allah, who fed us,
gave us drink, and made us Muslims.

DUA FOR GOODNESS IN THIS WORLD & THE HEREAFTER

When to Say It: Anytime, especially in Ramadan
when making *dua* is highly encouraged

رَبَّنَا آتِنَا فِي الدُّنْيَا حَسَنَةً وَفِي الْآخِرَةِ حَسَنَةً وَقِنَا عَذَابَ النَّارِ

Rabbana atina fi'd-dunya hasanata wa fi'l-akhirati hasanata wa qina 'adhab an-nar

Our Lord! Give us good in this world and good in the
Hereafter, and protect us from the punishment of the
Fire. (2:201)

DUA FOR STEADFASTNESS IN
PRAYER AND FORGIVENESS

When to Say It: During personal supplications

رَبِّ اجْعَلْنِي مُقِيمَ الصَّلَاةِ وَمِنْ ذُرِّيَّتِي رَبَّنَا وَتَقَبَّلْ دُعَاءِ
رَبَّنَا اغْفِرْ لِي وَلِوَالِدَيَّ وَلِلْمُؤْمِنِينَ يَوْمَ يَقُومُ الْحِسَابُ

*Rabbi ij'alni muqim al-salah wa min dhurriyati, rabbana wa
taqabbal du'a. Rabbana ighfir li wa li walidayya wa
li'l-mu'minin yawma yaqumu'l-hisab.*

My Lord! Make me steadfast in prayer, and also my
descendants. Our Lord! Accept my supplication.
Our Lord! Forgive me and my parents, and all the
Believers on the Day the Reckoning arises. (14:40-41)

DUA FOR JOY IN FAMILY &
EXEMPLARY LEADERSHIP

When to Say It: Regularly, to seek blessings for
your family and to aspire to goodness.

رَبَّنَا هَبْ لَنَا مِنْ أَزْوَاجِنَا وَذُرِّيَّاتِنَا قُرَّةَ أَعْيُنٍ وَاجْعَلْنَا لِلْمُتَّقِينَ إِمَامًا

*Rabbana hab lana min azwajina wa dhurriyatina
qurrata a'yun wa ij'alna li'l-muttaqina imama*

Our Lord! Grant us from our spouses and our
offspring comfort to our eyes, and make us an
example for the righteous. (25:74)

COMPREHENSIVE DUA FOR ALL GOOD AND PROTECTION FROM EVIL

When to Say It: In any moment of reflection
or during special nights in Ramadan.

اللَّهُمَّ إِنِّي أَسْأَلُكَ مِنَ الْخَيْرِ كُلِّهِ عَاجِلِهِ وَآجِلِهِ ، مَا عَلِمْتُ مِنْهُ
وَمَا لَمْ أَعْلَمْ ،وَأَعُوذُ بِكَ مِنَ الشَّرِّ كُلِّهِ عَاجِلِهِ وَآجِلِهِ

*Allahumma inni as'aluka min al-khayri kullihi
'ajilihi wa ajilihi, ma 'alimtu minhu wa ma lam a'lam...*

Oh Allah! I ask You for all good, immediate and
delayed, what I know of it and what I do not know.
And I seek refuge in You from all evil, immediate and
delayed, what I know of it and what I do not know...

DUA FOR PARDON AND WELL-BEING

When to Say It: Regularly, especially in
moments of seeking protection

اللَّهُمَّ إِنِّي أَسْأَلُكَ الْعَافِيَةَ فِي الدُّنْيَا وَالْآخِرَةِ

Allahumma inni as'aluka al-'afiyata fi'd-dunya wa'l-akhirah

Oh Allah! Indeed, I ask You for pardon
in this world and the Hereafter.

DUA FOR THE NIGHT
OF LAYLATUL QADR

Taught by the Prophet (SAW) to
Aisha (RA) for this blessed night.

اللَّهُمَّ إِنَّكَ عَفُوٌّ تُحِبُّ الْعَفْوَ فَاعْفُ عَنِّي

Allahumma innaka 'afuwwun tuhibbu'l-'afwa fa'fu 'anni

Oh Allah! Indeed, You are Pardoning,
You love to pardon, so pardon me.

DUA FOR FORGIVENESS

رَبِّ اغْفِرْ لِي وَتُبْ عَلَيَّ إِنَّكَ أَنْتَ التَّوَّابُ الرَّحِيمُ

Rabbi ighfir li wa tub 'alayya innaka anta'l-tawwabu'l-raheem

My Lord, forgive me and accept my repentance.
Indeed, You are the Accepting of repentance, the Merciful.

DUA FOR GRATITUDE AND GOOD HEALTH

اللَّهُمَّ إِنِّي أَسْأَلُكَ الْعَفْوَ وَالْعَافِيَةَ فِي دِينِي وَدُنْيَايَ وَأَهْلِي وَمَالِي

*Allahumma inni as'aluka al-'afwa wa al-'afiyata
fi deeni wa dunyaaya wa ahli wa maali.*

Oh Allah, I ask You for forgiveness and well-being
in my religious and worldly affairs, and for
my family and my wealth.

DUA FOR ACCEPTANCE OF DEEDS

رَبَّنَا تَقَبَّلْ مِنَّا إِنَّكَ أَنْتَ السَّمِيعُ الْعَلِيمُ

Rabbana taqabbal minna innaka anta al-samee'u al-'aleem

Our Lord, accept [this] from us.
Indeed, You are the Hearing, the Knowing. (2:127)

DUA FOR PROTECTION FROM HELLFIRE

اللَّهُمَّ أَجِرْنَا مِنَ النَّارِ

Allahumma ajirna minannaar

Oh Allah, protect us from the Fire.

DUA FOR EID TAKBEER
(RECITED DURING EID MORNING)

When to say it: It is Sunnah to recite the *takbeer*
starting from the night before Eid until the Eid prayer

اللهُ أَكْبَرُ، اللهُ أَكْبَرُ، اللهُ أَكْبَرُ
لَا إِلهَ إِلَّا اللهُ، اللهُ أَكْبَرُ، اللهُ أَكْبَرُ، وَلِلهِ الْحَمْدُ

Allahu Akbar, Allahu Akbar, Allahu Akbar, la ilaha illa Allah,
wallahu Akbar, Allahu Akbar, wa lillahi al-hamd

Allah is the Greatest, Allah is the Greatest, Allah is the Greatest,
there is no deity worthy of worship except Allah, Allah is the
Greatest, Allah is the Greatest, and all praise belongs to Allah.

My Personal Dua' List

A Special Place to Write Your Dua' During This Blessed Month

> *"And when My servants ask you concerning Me, indeed I am near. I respond to the invocation of the supplicant when he calls upon Me..."*
>
> —The Quran (2:186)

This chapter is a safe space for you to express your hopes, struggles, and dreams. It's your chance to pour your heart out and trust that Allah (SWT) hears you. You can use these specific *dua'* when opening your fast, during the last ten nights of Ramadan, or anytime, for that matter. As long as you are blessed with life, you have the opportunity to make *dua'*.

As humans, we are forgetful, so having your *dua'* written down can be a lifesaver! As you write out your list, ask yourself:

- What do I need most right now?
- What am I seeking in life?
- What do I hope for in the hereafter?
- Who in my life needs *dua'* right now?

Remember, Allah (SWT) is *Al-Samee'* (The All-Hearing). This name of His lets you know that He hears what is on your tongue *and* what is in your heart. May all your *dua'* be answered. Ameen.

The 99 Names of Allah (SWT)

A space to connect & reflect on the beautiful names & attributes of Allah (SWT)

Allah's name in Arabic	How to Say It	What It Means	Description
الرَّحْمَنُ	Ar-Rahman	The All-Compassionate	The most merciful, whose mercy extends to all of creation
الرَّحِيمُ	Ar-Rahim	The All-Merciful	The most kind, who shows compassion and forgiveness
الْمَلِكُ	Al-Malik	The Absolute Ruler	The ruler and sovereign, who governs the heavens and earth
الْقُدُّوسُ	Al-Quddus	The Pure One	The source of purity and sanctity; beyond any imperfection
السَّلَامُ	As-Salam	The Source of Peace	The one who grants peace and tranquility to all beings
الْمُؤْمِنُ	Al-Mu'min	The Inspirer of Faith	The one who provides safety, security, and the ability to believe
الْمُهَيْمِنُ	Al-Muhaymin	The Guardian	The one who watches over and protects all of creation
الْعَزِيزُ	Al-Aziz	The Victorious	The powerful and invincible one, who cannot be defeated
الْجَبَّارُ	Al-Jabbar	The Compeller	The one who has the power to repair and restore
الْمُتَكَبِّرُ	Al-Mutakabbir	The Greatest	The one who is exalted, above all creation, in majesty and grandeur
الْخَالِقُ	Al-Khaliq	The Creator	The one who brings everything into existence from nothing
الْبَارِئُ	Al-Bari'	The Maker of Order	The one who creates and shapes everything in its perfect form

Allah's name in Arabic	How to Say It	What It Means	Description
الْمُصَوِّرُ	Al-Musawwir	The Shaper of Beauty	The one who designs and forms all things with beauty and wisdom
الْغَفَّارُ	Al-Ghaffar	The Forgiving	The one who forgives the sins of all who repent, continually
الْقَهَّارُ	Al-Qahhar	The Subduer	The one who prevails over everything, compelling all things to follow His will
الْوَهَّابُ	Al-Wahhab	The Giver of All	The one who constantly gives and grants blessings without limits
الرَّزَّاقُ	Ar-Razzaq	The Sustainer	The one who provides sustenance and necessities to all of creation
الْفَتَّاحُ	Al-Fattah	The Opener	The one who opens the doors of mercy, guidance, and success
اَلْعَلِيْمُ	Al-'Alim	The Knower of All	The one who knows everything, past, present, and future
الْقَابِضُ	Al-Qabid	The Constrictor	The one who restrains and withholds blessings as He wills
الْبَاسِطُ	Al-Basit	The Reliever	The one who expands, increases, and grants abundance
الْخَافِضُ	Al-Khafid	The Abaser	The one who reduces and lowers the status of those He chooses
الرَّافِعُ	Ar-Rafi	The Exalter	The one who raises and elevates people to higher positions
الْمُعِزُّ	Al-Mu'izz	The Bestower of Honors	The one who honors and gives dignity and status to whom He wills
الْمُذِلُّ	Al-Mudhill	The Humiliator	The one who lowers, humbles, and degrades whom He chooses

Allah's name in Arabic	How to Say It	What It Means	Description
السَّمِيعُ	As-Sami	The Hearer of All	The one who hears all things, even the faintest sounds, perfectly
الْبَصِيرُ	Al-Basir	The Seer of All	The one who sees all things, even those hidden from our sight
الْحَكَمُ	Al-Hakam	The Judge	The one who judges fairly, without bias or injustice
الْعَدْلُ	Al-'Adl	The Just	The one who is perfectly just, ensuring fairness for all
اللَّطِيفُ	Al-Latif	The Subtle One	The one who acts with kindness and gentleness, even in subtle ways
الْخَبِيرُ	Al-Khabir	The All-Aware	The one who is fully aware of all things, inside and out
الْحَلِيمُ	Al-Halim	The Forbearing	The one who is patient and forgiving, even in the face of wrongdoing
الْعَظِيمُ	Al-Azim	The Magnificent	The one who is great, majestic, and awe-inspiring in every way
الْغَفُورُ	Al-Ghafur	The Forgiver and Hider of Faults	The one who forgives sins with great generosity and mercy
الشَّكُورُ	Ash-Shakur	The Rewarder of Thankfulness	The one who greatly rewards and appreciates even small acts of devotion
الْعَلِيُّ	Al-Ali	The Highest	The one who is exalted and raised above all things in grandeur
الْكَبِيرُ	Al-Kabir	The Greatest	The one who is grander than anything or anyone in existence

Allah's name in Arabic	How to Say It	What It Means	Description
الْحَفِيظُ	Al-Hafidh	The Preserver	The one who keeps, protects, and preserves everything in perfect order
الْمُقِيتُ	Al-Muqit	The Nourisher	The one who sustains and provides for all living things
الْحسِيبُ	Al-Hasib	The Accounter	The one who holds everyone accountable for their actions
الْجَلِيلُ	Al-Jalil	The Mighty	The one who is revered and has an imposing presence
الْكَرِيمُ	Al-Karim	The Generous	The one who gives abundantly, beyond measure
الرَّقِيبُ	Ar-Raqib	The Watchful One	The one who watches over and observes all things
الْمُجِيبُ	Al-Mujib	The Responder to Prayer	The one who responds to the calls of His servants
الْوَاسِعُ	Al-Wasi	The All-Comprehending	The one whose knowledge, mercy, and power encompass all things
الْحَكِيمُ	Al-Hakeem	The Perfectly Wise	The one who has complete wisdom and understanding in all matters
الْوَدُودُ	Al-Wadud	The Loving One	The one who loves His creation with perfect love
الْمَجِيدُ	Al-Majeed	The Majestic One	The one whose majesty and honor are beyond comprehension
الْبَاعِثُ	Al-Ba'ith	The Resurrector	The one who revives the dead and gives life

Allah's name in Arabic	How to Say It	What It Means	Description
الشَّهِيدُ	Ash-Shahid	The Witness	The one who is always present, witnessing everything
الْحَقُّ	Al-Haqq	The Truth	The one who is the absolute truth and the source of all truth
الْوَكِيلُ	Al-Wakil	The Trustee	The one who is relied upon, entrusted with all matters
الْقَوِيُّ	Al-Qawiyy	The Possessor of All Strength	The one who is the strongest and all-powerful
الْمَتِينُ	Al-Mateen	The Forceful One	The one who is strong, firm, and resolute
الْوَلِيُّ	Al-Waliyy	The Governor	The one who governs and protects His creation
الْحَمِيدُ	Al-Hameed	The Praised One	The one who is deserving of all praise
الْمُحْصِي	Al-Muhsi	The Appraiser	The one who counts and records all things
الْمُبْدِئُ	Al-Mubdi	The Originator	The one who initiates and originates everything from nothing
الْمُعِيدُ	Al-Mu'eed	The Restorer	The one who restores creation to its original state
الْمُحْيِي	Al-Muhyi	The Giver of Life	The one who gives life to the dead and sustains life
الْمُمِيتُ	Al-Mumit	The Taker of Life	The one who causes death and takes life away

Allah's name in Arabic	How to Say It	What It Means	Description
الْحَيُّ	Al-Hayy	The Ever Living One	The one who is eternally alive and whose existence has no end
الْقَيُّومُ	Al-Qayyum	The Self-Existing One	The one who is independent of all and sustains everything
الْوَاجِدُ	Al-Waajid	The Finder	The one who finds and brings forth what is needed
الْمَاجِدُ	Al-Maajid	The Glorious	The one who is full of glory, honor, and magnificence
الْوَاحِدُ	Al-Waahid	The Only One	The one who has no partner and is unique in all His attributes
اَلْأَحَدُ	Al-Ahad	The One	The one who is indivisible and without any equal
الصَّمَدُ	As-Samad	The Satisfier of All Needs	The one who fulfills all needs and desires of His creation
الْقَادِرُ	Al-Qadir	The All-Powerful	The one who has power over all things and can do anything
الْمُقْتَدِرُ	Al-Muqtadir	The Creator of All Power	The one who is capable of anything and is the creator of all power
الْمُقَدِّمُ	Al-Muqaddim	The Expediter	The one who advances and makes things happen in the right time
الْمُؤَخِّرُ	Al-Mu'akhkhir	The Delayer	The one who delays things, as He wills
الْأَوَّلُ	Al-Awwal	The First	The one who has no beginning and is the first in all things

Allah's name in Arabic	How to Say It	What It Means	Description
الآخِرُ	Al-Akhir	The Last	The one who has no end and is the last in all things
الظَّاهِرُ	Adh-dhahir	The Manifest One	The one who is outwardly apparent and visible in His greatness
الْبَاطِنُ	Al-Batin	The Hidden One	The one who is hidden from sight, yet present everywhere
الْوَالِي	Al-Wali	The Protecting Friend	The one who protects and guards His creation
الْمُتَعَالِي	Al-Muta'ali	The Supreme One	The one who is exalted and supreme over all creation
الْبَرُّ	Al-Barr	The Doer of Good	The one who does good for His creation and guides them to righteousness
التَّوَّابُ	At-Tawwab	The Guide to Repentance	The one who accepts repentance and forgives sins
الْمُنْتَقِمُ	Al-Muntaqim	The Avenger	The one who avenges wrongs and acts with justice
الْعَفُوُّ	Al-'Afuww	The Forgiver	The one who pardons and forgives the faults of His creation
الرَّؤُوفُ	Ar-Ra'uf	The Clement	The one who is merciful, kind, and gentle towards His creation
مَالِكُ الْمُلْكِ	Malik-ul-Mulk	The Owner of All	The one who possesses the dominion of the heavens and earth
ذُو الْجَلَالِ وَ الإكْرَامِ	Dhu-al-Jalal wal-Ikram	The Lord of Majesty and Bounty	The one who is supreme in majesty and generosity

Allah's name in Arabic	How to Say It	What It Means	Description
الْمُقْسِطُ	Al-Muqsit	The Equitable One	The one who ensures justice is maintained in all affairs
الْجَامِعُ	Al-Jami'	The Gatherer	The one who gathers His creation and all their needs
ألْغَنِيُّ	Al-Ghaniyy	The Self-Sufficient	The one who is not in need of anyone or anything
الْمُغْنِي	Al-Mughni	The Enricher	The one who enriches and provides abundance to His creation
المانع	Al-Mani'	The Preventer	The one who prevents harm or difficulty as He wills
الضَّار	Adh-Dharr	The Afflicter	The one who brings adversity when needed
النَّافِع	An-Nafi'	The Benefactor	The one who provides good and benefit to His creation
النُّور	An-Nur	The Light	The one who is the source of all light in creation
الهادي	Al-Haadi	The Guide	The one who leads His creation to righteousness
البديع	Al-Badee'	The Originator	The one who creates something new without any prior example
الباقي	Al-Baqi	The Everlasting	The one who is eternal and will remain forever
الوارث	Al-Warith	The Inheritor of All	The one who inherits all creation

Allah's name in Arabic	How to Say It	What It Means	Description
الرشيد	*Ar-Rasheed*	The Rightly Guided	The one who guides His creation to the correct path
الصبور	As-Saboor	The Patient	The one who is infinitely patient with His creation

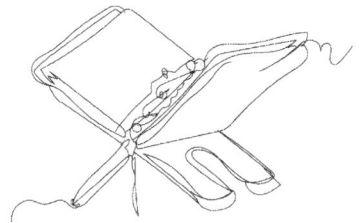

My Quran Reading Log

A Space to Track Your Daily Recitation Goals & to Ponder Upon the Meanings of The Quran

> *"And when the Quran is recited, then listen to it and pay attention that you may receive mercy."*
>
> —The Quran (7:204)

Ramadan is the month in which the Quran was revealed. Therefore, a great deal of our worship in this month should gravitate around the recitation of Allah's (SWT) book. In Surah Al-Baqarah, Allah (SWT) tells us: *"The month of Ramadan [is that] in which was revealed the Quran, a guidance for the people and clear proofs of guidance and criterion."* (2:185). This is a reminder that during this blessed month, our connection to the Quran should be at the forefront of our worship.

As you set your Quran reading goals for this month, I want you to remember that true success cannot be achieved just from the recitation of the Quran alone. *Your goal must be deeper than this.* You should set out to understand the meaning of the words you recite, and to internalize them. By understanding and reflecting on the guidance Allah (SWT) provides for us in the Quran, we can then begin to apply it to our lives.

For years I had prioritized recitation over reflection. However, it was only when I made it an intention to *slow down*, and understand what I was reciting, that the Quran began to manifest through my actions. There is a powerful transformation that can only occur in your heart and mind when you take the time to connect with the meanings of Allah's (SWT) words. So my sincere advice to you this Ramadan (and beyond) is to take the time to ponder the verses, seek understanding, and allow this new wisdom to shape your actions.

This month is a reminder that the Quran is more than a book—it is the ultimate guide for our lives. Through it, we can find answers to our challenges, comfort for our hearts, and clarity for our purpose.

In this section of your Ramadan Journal, you'll find space to track your daily Quran recitation. Additionally, there is a dedicated area for reflecting on the verses you read, allowing you to note any insights or lessons that resonate with you. Let this practice deepen your connection with the Quran and enrich your Ramadan experience.

May Allah (SWT) make this journey of recitation and reflection a source of growth for you, and may the Quran be a light and witness for you on the Day of Judgment. *Ameen.*

"I am leaving among you two precious things, and if you adhere to both of them, you will never go astray after me. They are the Book of Allah and my Sunnah."

—Prophet Muhammad (SAW)
[Muslim]

NOTE: IF YOUR GOAL IS TO COMPLETE READING THE ENTIRE QURAN DURING RAMADAN, THE CHAPTERS IN THE TABLE ARE EVENLY DIVIDED WITH THE CORRECT START AND END POINTS FOR EACH DAY. THIS WILL HELP YOU PACE YOUR RECITATION EVENLY THROUGHOUT THE MONTH. IF YOU AIM TO FINISH MORE OR LESS THAN THE FULL QURAN, FEEL FREE TO ADJUST YOUR GOALS TO FIT YOUR PERSONAL PLAN.

Ch.	Juzz	Arabic Name	How to Say It	English Meaning	R READ	M MEMORIZE	I IMPLEMENT
1	1	الفاتحة	Al-Fatiha	The Opening			
2	1	البقرة	Al-Baqarah	The Cow			
3	1	آل عمران	Aali Imran	The Family of Imran			
4	1	النساء	An-Nisa	The Women			
5	2	المائدة	Al-Ma'idah	The Table Spread			
6	2	الأنعام	Al-An'am	The Cattle			
7	2	الأعراف	Al-A'raf	The Elevated Place			
8	2	الأنفال	Al-Anfal	The Spoils of War			
9	2	التوبة	At-Tawbah	The Repentance			
10	3	يونس	Yunus	Jonah			
11	3	هود	Hud	Hud			
12	3	يوسف	Yusuf	Joseph			
13	3	الرعد	Ar-Ra'd	The Thunder			
14	3	إبراهيم	Ibrahim	Abraham			
15	3	الحجر	Al-Hijr	The Rocky Tract			
16	4	النحل	An-Nahl	The Bee			
17	4	الإسراء	Al-Isra	The Night Journey			
18	4	الكهف	Al-Kahf	The Cave			

Ch.	Juzz	Arabic Name	How to Say It	English Meaning	R READ	M MEMORIZE	I IMPLEMENT
19	4	مريم	Maryam	Mary			
20	4	طه	Ta-Ha	Ta-Ha			
21	5	الأنبياء	Al-Anbiya	The Prophets			
22	5	الحج	Al-Hajj	The Pilgrimage			
23	5	المؤمنون	Al-Mu'minun	The Believers			
24	5	النور	An-Nur	The Light			
25	6	الفرقان	Al-Furqan	The Criterion			
26	6	الشعراء	Ash-Shu'ara	The Poets			
27	6	النمل	An-Naml	The Ant			
28	6	القصص	Al-Qasas	The Stories			
29	7	العنكبوت	Al-Ankabut	The Spider			
30	7	الروم	Ar-Rum	The Romans			
31	7	لقمان	Luqman	Luqman			
32	7	السجدة	As-Sajda	The Prostration			
33	8	الأحزاب	Al-Ahzab	The Confederates			
34	8	سبأ	Saba	Sheba			
35	8	فاطر	Fatir	The Originator			
37	9	الصافات	As-Saffat	Those who set the ranks			

Ch.	Juzz	Arabic Name	How to Say It	English Meaning	R READ	M MEMORIZE	I IMPLEMENT
38	9	ص	Sad	Sad			
39	10	الزمر	Az-Zumar	The Troops			
40	10	غافر	Ghafir	The Forgiver			
41	10	فصلت	Fussilat	Explained in Detail			
42	10	الشورى	Ash-Shura	The Consultation			
43	11	الزخرف	Az-Zukhruf	The Gold Adornments			
44	11	الدخان	Ad-Dukhan	The Smoke			
45	11	الجاثية	Al-Jathiya	The Kneeling Down			
46	11	الأحقاف	Al-Ahqaf	The Sand-Dunes			
47	11	محمد	Muhammad	Muhammad			
48	12	الفتح	Al-Fath	The Conquest			
49	12	الحجرات	Al-Hujurat	The Private Apartments			
50	12	ق	Qaf	Qaf			
51	13	الذاريات	Adh-Dhariyat	The Dust-Scattering Winds			
52	13	الطور	At-Tur	The Mount			
53	13	النجم	An-Najm	The Star			
54	13	القمر	Al-Qamar	The Moon			
55	14	الرحمن	Ar-Rahman	The Most Merciful			
56	14	الواقعة	Al-Waqi'a	The Inevitable			

Ch.	Juzz	Arabic Name	How to Say It	English Meaning	R READ	M MEMORIZE	I IMPLEMENT
57	14	الحديد	Al-Hadid	Iron			
58	14	المجادلة	Al-Mujadila	The Pleading Woman			
59	14	الحشر	Al-Hashr	The Gathering			
60	15	الممتحنة	Al-Mumtahina	The Examined One			
61	15	الصف	As-Saff	The Ranks			
62	15	الجمعة	Al-Jumu'a	Congregation			
63	15	المنافقون	Al-Munafiqun	The Hypocrites			
64	15	التغابن	At-Taghabun	The Cheating			
65	15	الطلاق	At-Talaq	Divorce			
66	15	التحريم	At-Tahrim	The Prohibition			
67	16	الملك	Al-Mulk	The Dominion			
68	16	القلم	Al-Qalam	The Pen			
69	16	الحاقة	Al-Haqqah	The Sure Reality			
70	16	المعارج	Al-Maarij	The Ascending Stairways			
71	16	نوح	Nuh	Noah			
72	17	الجن	Al-Jinn	The Jinn			
73	17	المزمل	Al-Muzzammil	The Enshrouded One			
74	17	المدثر	Al-Muddathir	The Cloaked One			

Ch.	Juzz	Arabic Name	How to Say It	English Meaning	R READ	M MEMORIZE	I IMPLEMENT
75	17	القيامة	Al-Qiyama	The Day of Resurrection			
76	17	الإنسان	Al-Insan	The Human			
77	17	المرسلات	Al-Mursalat	The Emissaries			
78	18	النبأ	An-Naba	The Great News			
79	18	النازعات	An-Nazi'at	Those Who Tear Out			
80	18	عبس	Abasa	He Frowned			
81	18	التكوير	At-Takwir	The Overthrowing			
82	18	الإنفطار	Al-Infitar	The Bursting Apart			
83	18	المطففين	Al-Mutaffifin	The Dealers in Fraud			
84	18	الإنشقاق	Al-Inshiqaq	The Splitting Open			
85	18	البروج	Al-Buruj	The Constellations			
86	18	الطارق	At-Tariq	The Morning Star			
87	18	الأعلى	Al-A'la	The Most High			
88	18	الغاشية	Al-Ghashiya	The Overwhelming Event			
89	19	الفجر	Al-Fajr	The Daybreak			
90	19	البلد	Al-Balad	The City			
91	19	الشمس	Ash-Shams	The Sun			
92	19	الليل	Al-Lail	The Night			

Ch.	Juzz	Arabic Name	How to Say It	English Meaning	R READ	M MEMORIZE	I IMPLEMENT
93	19	الضحى	Adh-Dhuha	The Forenoon			
94	19	الشرح	Ash-Sharh	The Relief			
95	19	التين	At-Tin	The Fig			
96	19	العلق	Al-Alaq	The Clot of Blood			
97	20	القدر	Al-Qadr	The Night of Power			
98	20	البينة	Al-Bayyina	The Clear Evidence			
99	20	الزلزلة	Az-Zalzalah	The Earthquake			
100	20	العديات	Al-Adiyat	The War Horse			
101	20	القارعة	Al-Qari'a	The Striking Hour			
102	20	التكاثر	At-Takathur	The Piling Up			
103	20	العصر	Al-Asr	The Time			
104	20	الهمزة	Al-Humazah	The Slanderer			
105	20	الفيل	Al-Fil	The Elephant			
106	20	قريش	Quraish	Quraish			
107	20	الماعون	Al-Ma'un	The Small Kindnesses			
108	20	الكوثر	Al-Kawthar	The Abundance			
109	20	الكافرون	Al-Kafirun	The Disbelievers			
110	20	النصر	An-Nasr	The Divine Support			

Ch.	Juzz	Arabic Name	How to Say It	English Name	R READ	M MEMORIZE	I IMPLEMENT
111	20	المسد	Al-Masad	The Palm Fiber			
112	20	الإخلاص	Al-Ikhlas	The Purity of Faith			
113	20	الفلق	Al-Falaq	The Daybreak			
114	20	الناس	An-Nas	Mankind			

surah

CHECKLIST

- ○ 1. Al-Fatiha
- ○ 2. Al-Baqarah
- ○ 3. Aali Imran
- ○ 4. An-Nisa'
- ○ 5. Al-Ma'idah
- ○ 6. Al-An'am
- ○ 7. Al-A'raf
- ○ 8. Al-Anfal
- ○ 9. At-Tawbah
- ○ 10. Yunus
- ○ 11. Hud
- ○ 12. Yusuf
- ○ 13. Ar-Ra'd
- ○ 14. Ibrahim
- ○ 15. Al-Hijr
- ○ 16. An-Nahl
- ○ 17. Al-Isra'
- ○ 18. Al-Kahf
- ○ 19. Maryam
- ○ 20. Ta-Ha
- ○ 21. Al-Anbiya
- ○ 22. Al-Hajj
- ○ 23. Al-Mu'minun
- ○ 24. An-Nur
- ○ 25. Al-Furqan
- ○ 26. Ash-Shu'ara
- ○ 27. An-Naml
- ○ 28. Al-Qasas
- ○ 29. Al-Ankabut

- ○ 30. Ar-Rum
- ○ 31. Luqman
- ○ 32. As-Sajda
- ○ 33. Al-Ahzab
- ○ 34. Saba
- ○ 35. Fatir
- ○ 36. Ya-Sin
- ○ 37. As-Saffat
- ○ 38. Sad
- ○ 39. Az-Zumar
- ○ 40. Ghafir
- ○ 41. Fussilat
- ○ 42. Ash-Shura
- ○ 43. Az-Zukhruf
- ○ 44. Ad-Dukhan
- ○ 45. Al-Jathiya
- ○ 46. Al-Ahqaf
- ○ 47. Muhammad
- ○ 48. Al-Fath
- ○ 49. Al-Hujurat
- ○ 50. Qaf
- ○ 51. Adh-Dhariyat
- ○ 52. At-Tur
- ○ 53. An-Najm
- ○ 54. Al-Qamar
- ○ 55. Ar-Rahman
- ○ 56. Al-Waqi'ah
- ○ 57. Al-Hadid
- ○ 58. Al-Mujadila

- ○ 59. Al-Hashr
- ○ 60. Al-Mumtahina
- ○ 61. As-Saff
- ○ 62. Al-Jumu'ah
- ○ 63. Al-Munafiqun
- ○ 64. At-Taghabun
- ○ 65. At-Talaq
- ○ 66. At-Tahrim
- ○ 67. Al-Mulk
- ○ 68. Al-Qalam
- ○ 69. Al-Haqqah
- ○ 70. Al-Maarij
- ○ 71. Nuh
- ○ 72. Al-Jinn
- ○ 73. Al-Muzzammil
- ○ 74. Al-Muddathir
- ○ 75. Al-Qiyamah
- ○ 76. Al-Insan
- ○ 77. Al-Mursalat
- ○ 78. An-Naba
- ○ 79. An-Nazi'at
- ○ 80. Abasa
- ○ 81. At-Takwir
- ○ 82. Al-Infitar
- ○ 83. Al-Mutaffifin
- ○ 84. Al-Inshiqaq
- ○ 85. Al-Buruj
- ○ 86. At-Tariq
- ○ 87. Al-A'la

- ○ 88. Al-Ghashiyah
- ○ 89. Al-Fajr
- ○ 90. Al-Balad
- ○ 91. Ash-Shams
- ○ 92. Al-Lail
- ○ 93. Adh-Dhuha
- ○ 94. Ash-Sharh
- ○ 95. At-Tin
- ○ 96. Al-Alaq
- ○ 97. Al-Qadr
- ○ 98. Al-Bayyina
- ○ 99. Az-Zalzalah
- ○ 100. Al-Adiyat
- ○ 101. Al-Qariah
- ○ 102. At-Takathur
- ○ 103. Al-Asr
- ○ 104. Al-Humazah
- ○ 105. Al-Fil
- ○ 106. Quraish
- ○ 107. Al-Ma'un
- ○ 108. Al-Kawthar
- ○ 109. Al-Kafirun
- ○ 110. An-Nasr
- ○ 111. Al-Masad
- ○ 112. Al-Ikhlas
- ○ 113. Al-Falaq
- ○ 114. An-Nas

My Quran
Reflection Journal

Use this section to jot down your thoughts and reflections on the verses you read. Instead of just reading, pause to think about what the verses mean to you and how they apply to your life. This is your chance to make the Quran's teachings personal to you. Remember, it's not just about reciting—it's about reflecting, understanding, and applying what you read to your life.

REFERENCE	VERSE	REFLECTION	ACTIONABLE TAKEAWAY
write down the surah & ayah no.	*write the translation of the verse that stood out to you*	*why does this verse resonate with you?*	*how can you apply this in your life?*

REFERENCE	VERSE	REFLECTION	ACTIONABLE TAKEAWAY
write down the surah & ayah no.	*write the translation of the verse that stood out to you*	*why does this verse resonate with you?*	*how can you apply this in your life?*

REFERENCE	VERSE	REFLECTION	ACTIONABLE TAKEAWAY
write down the surah & ayah no.	*write the translation of the verse that stood out to you*	*why does this verse resonate with you?*	*how can you apply this in your life?*

REFERENCE	VERSE	REFLECTION	ACTIONABLE TAKEAWAY
write down the surah & ayah no.	*write the translation of the verse that stood out to you*	*why does this verse resonate with you?*	*how can you apply this in your life?*

REFERENCE	VERSE	REFLECTION	ACTIONABLE TAKEAWAY
write down the surah & ayah no.	*write the translation of the verse that stood out to you*	*why does this verse resonate with you?*	*how can you apply this in your life?*

REFERENCE	VERSE	REFLECTION	ACTIONABLE TAKEAWAY
write down the surah & ayah no.	*write the translation of the verse that stood out to you*	*why does this verse resonate with you?*	*how can you apply this in your life?*

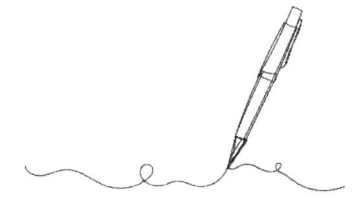

My Habit
Tracker

Before Ramadan begins, think about the habits you want to build and those you want to leave behind. By assessing what you want to do more of—like praying, reading Quran, or being kind—and what you want to cut out—like procrastination or bad thoughts—you can be more intentional with your time during the month. Doing this ahead of time will help you make the most of Ramadan, so you can grow spiritually and be closer to Allah (SWT).

HABIT TRACKER

Use this daily habit tracker to monitor your progress in building positive habits and letting go of unhelpful ones throughout Ramadan. Research shows it takes just 21 days to establish a habit, making Ramadan the perfect time to create lasting changes for the rest of the year.

day	reduce screen time to 30 mins a day						
1							
2							
3							
4							
5							
6							
7							
8							
9							
10							
11							
12							
13							
14							
15							
16							
17							
18							
19							
20							
21							
22							
23							
24							
25							
26							
27							
28							
29							
30							

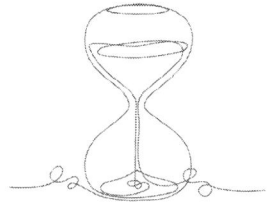

My Ramadan Reflections

To prepare for this Ramadan, I want you to take a moment to think back on your experiences from last year. How has the past year shaped you? In this section, you'll find writing prompts to help you reflect on your journey—your challenges, your wins, and everything in between. This isn't about feeling guilty or dwelling on what didn't go perfectly; it's about learning from where you have been and carrying those lessons into this Ramadan with purpose and a positive mindset. Let's get started.

What were some important things I learned last Ramadan?

How can I use them to get closer to Allah (SWT) this year?

Did I reach my goals last Ramadan?

If not, what made it hard? How can I do better this time?

What kind deeds did I do for others last Ramadan?

How did it make me feel? How can I do even more acts of kindness this year?

Did I feel like I had too much to do last Ramadan?

How can I make time for everything this year without feeling stressed?

How did I spend time with my community last Ramadan?

What can I do to stay connected or meet new people this year?

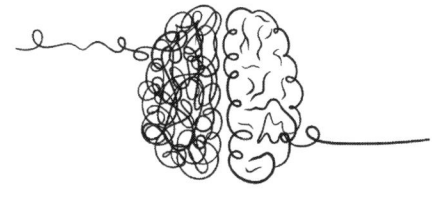

RAMADAN REFRAME

Conquer Your Limiting Beliefs
& Build a Growth Mindset
About Ramadan

> *"Allah has said, 'Every deed of the son of Adam is for him except fasting; it is for Me, and I will reward it.'"*
>
> —Prophet Muhammad (SAW)
> [Bukhari 5927]

Ramadan is a month many of us eagerly await. It offers beautiful opportunities to reflect on our lives with gratitude, strengthen our connection with family, and renew our *eman* as it fluctuates throughout the year.

However, while we cherish this blessed time, it is natural to feel physical, emotional, and mental strain as we balance worship with family, work, and other responsibilities. Allah (SWT) understands this, yet He has commanded us to observe fasting during this month because of its immense benefits. Allah (SWT) says in the Quran:

"...but to fast is best for you, if you only knew."

—The Quran (2:184)

Keeping this in mind as we navigate through Ramadan can help us maintain our momentum. In psychology, this technique is called a "reframe." A reframe is a mental shift that motivates us to look at a challenge or limiting belief in a way that encourages us to stay engaged and focused. *It's a powerful skill to have.*

As a mother, you might feel like you're constantly juggling the responsibility of preparing *suhoor* and *iftar*, helping the kids with their homework, and still trying to squeeze in time for worship. If you're married or living with family, you might find yourself prioritizing everyone else's needs, while secretly hoping for a quiet moment to connect with Allah (SWT). And if you're also managing work and other commitments, the weight of it all can feel even heavier.

You might catch yourself thinking, "Am I doing enough worship?" or "Why is fasting so hard for me?" The good news is that you are not alone in these feelings. Many of us face similar struggles during this blessed month. By acknowledging these thoughts, you are already taking the first step toward overcoming them.

I often discuss with my clients how limiting beliefs can hold us back from experiencing life to its fullest. When we feel the need to be perfect in our *ibaadah* or believe that we are unworthy of Allah's (SWT) mercy, it creates unnecessary pressure—especially during Ramadan. I don't want that to stop you from embracing the beauty of this blessed month.

Remember, just as we work to challenge these beliefs in therapy, we can apply the same practice to our spiritual journey. My sister, Islam was made easy, but sometimes, we overcomplicate it for ourselves. The Prophet (SAW) told us:

"Indeed, this religion is easy, and no one will ever overburden himself in religion, except that it will overcome him. So seek what is appropriate, and come as close as you can, and receive the glad tidings (that you will be rewarded), and take it easy; and gain strength by worshipping in the mornings, afternoons, and during the last hours of the nights."

—The Prophet Muhammad (SAW)
[An-Nasa'i 5034]

As we can see from the divinely inspired words of Rasulullah (SAW), the best path is one of moderation. So, if you ever find yourself thinking, "I didn't pray enough *nawafil* today, so I must be failing," try reframing that thought to: "I made an effort to pray additional prayers, and every moment spent in worship—especially extra acts, no matter how small—is valued by Allah (SWT)."

By recognizing that our worth is not solely defined by our performance but more importantly by our intentions and efforts, we can relieve ourselves from the unnecessary pressure we often place on our own shoulders.

In this section, we'll explore some common thoughts and challenges that might arise during Ramadan. Then, we'll reframe these thoughts so that they don't become obstacles to our success. Instead, this reframe will empower and motivate you as you do your best during this blessed month.

Finally, remind yourself that every step you take toward Allah (SWT)—*especially* the difficult ones—is an opportunity to draw closer to Him. May you enjoy the blessings of this holy month. *Ameen.*

Shift Your Perspective

WHAT'S WEIGHING ON YOU?	YOUR INITIAL THOUGHT MIGHT BE...	NOW POSITIVELY REFRAME IT BY SAYING...	SOME-THING TO REFLECT ON..
I'm struggling to complete my 5 daily prayers on time	"I'm falling behind on my prayers, and it feels like I'm failing in my worship this Ramadan."	"Even though I've missed some prayers, I can make sincere efforts to improve and ask Allah (SWT) for forgiveness. Every step toward fulfilling my prayers is a step closer to Allah (SWT)."	Allah (SWT) is Most Forgiving: "Indeed, Allah loves those who are constantly repentant..." —The Quran (2:222)
I'm feel-ing over-whelmed with fasting and work	"Balancing work and fasting feels impossible; I'm exhausted."	"This exhaustion is a temporary test, and through it, I'm purifying myself spiritually. With every moment of fatigue, Allah (SWT) is rewarding me for my efforts."	Reward of Fasting: "Fasting is for Me, and I will give the reward for it." [Bukhari 5927]
I'm unable to focus during *taraweeh* prayer	"My mind keeps wandering during *taraweeh*, and I feel like I'm not getting the full benefit of the prayer."	"It's okay to struggle with focus. I'll take small steps, like setting a clear intention before praying and focusing on one *surah*. Even trying my best is valuable to Allah (SWT)."	Intention Matters: "Actions are judged by intentions." [Bukhari 1]

WHAT'S WEIGHING ON YOU?	YOUR INITIAL THOUGHT MIGHT BE…	NOW POSITIVELY REFRAME IT BY SAYING…	SOME-THING TO REFLECT ON..
I'm feeling disconnected from the spiritual aspects of Ramadan	"I don't feel spiritually connected this Ramadan, and it's making me feel guilty."	"Spirituality has its highs and lows. Even if I don't feel it now, my efforts to seek closeness to Allah (SWT) will bear fruit over time. I trust the process."	Trust in the Process: "And whoever is mindful of Allah—He will make a way out for them." —The Quran (65:2)
I'm struggling to read the Quran every day	"I'm falling behind on my Quran recitation, and I don't think I'll finish in time for Ramadan."	"Even if I don't finish the entire Quran, every verse I read is a source of light and guidance. It's about consistency and sincerity, not the speed."	Reward in Every Effort: "Whoever recites a letter from the Book of Allah, he will receive one good deed as ten." [Tirmidhi 2910]
I'm not able to do as much ibadah due to family responsibilities	"I wish I could do more acts of worship, but family responsibilities are holding me back."	"Caring for my family is also an act of worship. Allah (SWT) knows my circumstances, and He rewards me for serving those around me with love and patience."	Multiple Paths to Worship: "The best of you are those who are best to their families." [Bukhari]

WHAT'S WEIGHING ON YOU?	YOUR INITIAL THOUGHT MIGHT BE…	NOW POSITIVELY REFRAME IT BY SAYING…	SOME-THING TO REFLECT ON..
I have to constantly attend to my children when I'm fasting	"I'm so tired from fasting, and my children's constant needs make it hard to find peace."	"Attending to my children is a way of serving Allah (SWT). Every moment of patience I show is an opportunity to gain reward, especially during Ramadan."	Patience is Worship: "Verily, with hardship comes ease." —The Quran (94:6)
I'm unable to attend *taraweeh* due to caring for my young children	"I wish I could go to the mosque for *taraweeh* like everyone else, but I have to stay home to care for my young children."	"Allah (SWT) rewards me for my intention and my role as a mother and wife. I can make *taraweeh* at home, and my devotion will still be counted, inshaAllah."	Intentions Matter: "Indeed, actions are according to intentions." [Bukhari 1]
I'm feel-ing over-whelmed with prepar-ing *iftar*	"I'm spending so much time in the kitchen, and I feel like I'm missing out on more important acts of worship."	"Preparing i*ftar* for my family is also an act of worship. Every meal I prepare with the intention of feeding others for the sake of Allah (SWT) is rewarded."	Feeding Others in Ramadan: "Whoever gives food to a fasting person to break his fast will have a reward like theirs." [Tirmidhi 807]

Positive Affirmations for Ramadan

Positive affirmations are a powerful way to shift our thinking from negative to positive. By consciously choosing uplifting thoughts, we can train our minds to face challenges with this life-changing habit. In this section, you'll find a collection of affirmations specifically for Ramadan. Each one is designed to inspire you and remind you of the beautiful journey you're on. Take a moment to reflect on what these affirmations mean to you personally and try incorporating them into your daily routine—especially on tougher days. Remember, every small effort you make during Ramadan is meaningful in the eyes of Allah (SWT). You are capable of so much, and this month is an opportunity to grow, shine, and excel.

I want you to remind yourself…

"I am nurturing my soul and my family
through my devotion this Ramadan."

"I embrace the challenges of motherhood
with patience and grace."

"My efforts in caring for my family
are a form of worship."

"I find strength in my *deen* to guide
me through each day of fasting."

"I am grateful for the opportunity to create
meaningful memories with my loved ones."

"Each *salah* I offer brings me closer to Allah (SWT)
and strengthens my family bond."

"I am deserving of self-care and moments
of rest during this holy month."

"My love and support uplift my family,
helping us grow closer together."

"I trust in Allah's (SWT) plan for me and
my family during Ramadan and beyond."

"I approach the challenges of fasting
with a heart full of gratitude."

"I am capable of managing my responsibilities
while nurturing my *eman*."

"Every small act of kindness I show my family is a
step toward receiving Allah's (SWT) mercy."

"I celebrate the joy of sharing *iftar*
and *suhoor* with my loved ones."

"I embrace the quiet moments of reflection and
dua as opportunities for growth."

"I am a role model for my children,
showing them the beauty of Islam-in-action."

"I honor my feelings and give myself
grace when things feel overwhelming."

"I choose to focus on the blessings of Ramadan
rather than the challenges."

"I am surrounded by love and support
from my family and community."

"I trust in my ability to nurture my family's
spirituality as well as my own."

"This Ramadan, I will allow myself to be present and mindful of the blessings Allah (SWT) has gifted and tested me with."

Productivity Hacks

Strategies to Enhance Barakah in Your Time & Achieve Your Goals

> *"The most beloved deeds to Allah are those that are done consistently, even if they are small."*
>
> —The Prophet Muhammad (SAW)
> [Ibn Majah 4327]

Ramadan is a time of profound spiritual elevation, self-discipline, and reflection, where the reward for every act of worship is multiplied. However, in today's fast-paced world, the demands of modern life—family obligations, work, and digital distractions—can make it difficult to focus on our spiritual goals and work effectively for our *akhirah*.

With the endless stream of notifications from social media apps and the constant pinging of messages, it's easy to feel our attention scattered. This makes the question of how to manage our time, focus, and energy effectively during Ramadan even more critical.

Throughout history, scholars and righteous Muslims have been celebrated for their ability to maximize their time during Ramadan, achieving extraordinary feats of worship, learning, and service. They attributed their success to the *barakah* (blessing) in their time, which they sought through intentional focus on acts of devotion.

For instance, Imam al-Shafi'i—known for his deep connection with the Quran—was said to recite the entire Quran sixty times during Ramadan, dedicating himself to its recitation both in his prayers and outside of them. Similarly, Imam Ibn Rajab al-Hanbali exemplified spiritual devotion during this blessed month. He would spend long nights in *tahajjud* (the night prayer), reciting the Quran, and immersing himself in personal acts of worship. It is narrated that he set aside all other commitments to fully devote himself to increasing his worship during Ramadan, serving as an inspiring example of dedication.

You might be wondering: *How can I compete with such devotion when I have so many distractions and so little time?* I want you to remember that the concept of *barakah* is not beyond your reach. It is accessible to anyone who approaches Ramadan with intentionality, focus, and a desire to earn Allah's (SWT) pleasure.

In this chapter, you will find 50 practical tried-and-tested productivity hacks that will not only help you manage your time more efficiently but will also allow you to invite *barakah* into your days. From setting clear spiritual goals to simplifying your daily routines, these tips will guide you in conserving energy, boosting your focus, and making the most of every minute of Ramadan. Whether you're balancing motherhood, work, or other personal responsibilities, these hacks will empower you to organize your time so that you can stay spiritually connected, energized, and mindful throughout this important month.

As a Muslim wife and mother, your influence shapes the family dynamic during Ramadan. Your intentions and dedication set the tone for the household, turning this sacred month into a time of *shared* spirituality. By incorporating tips such as meal planning, involving your children in acts of worship, and establishing a family schedule, you can create a nurturing environment that acts as the bedrock for spiritual growth for everyone.

Additionally, involving your children in worship transforms Ramadan into a family affair, strengthening bonds and teaching them valuable lessons about kindness and charity. By making these practices a part of your family routine, you will also instill lasting values in your children.

As you implement these tips, you will begin to see how much can be accomplished when your time is blessed with *barakah*. Remember, Ramadan is a rare and unique opportunity that comes only once a year. Use these strategies thoughtfully, and you'll naturally experience the blessings that result from the investment you make in both your spiritual *and* personal growth.

Spiritual & Personal Growth Tips

SET CLEAR INTENTIONS DAILY
Begin each day by setting specific spiritual and personal goals with the right intention for Allah's (SWT) sake.

USE A PRAYER AND QURAN TRACKER
Track your salah and Quran recitation throughout the month to make sure you are being consistent and making progress (both trackers are included in this Ramadan Journal).

SET 3 SPIRITUAL GOALS
Identify three key spiritual goals (e.g., completing the Quran, increasing dhikr, or improving character) and focus on actionable steps to achieve them.

UTILIZE QUIET TIME FOR WORSHIP
Use early mornings or the kid's nap times to focus on personal worship, like Quran recitation, *dua*, or *salah*.

PREPARE YOUR DUA LIST AHEAD OF LAYLATUL QADR
Write down your *dua*' in advance for the last ten nights of Ramadan, focusing especially on *Laylatul Qadr*. This will help you stay organized and maximize your supplications during this rewarding time.

STAY CONSISTENT
Reflect daily on your spiritual progress and make necessary adjustments to stay on track.

Family & Community Engagement Tips

TEACH KIDS THE MEANING OF RAMADAN
Engage your children in charitable deeds like distributing food or donating toys to teach them the importance of giving.

SET FAMILY IBADAH GOALS
Set collective family goals for Ramadan, such as reflecting on the Quran together and praying *taraweeh* as a family.

VOLUNTEER LOCALLY
Set aside time to volunteer at a local charity.

PLAN RAMADAN ACTIVITIES FOR KIDS
Organize crafts, stories, or learning sessions about Ramadan to keep children engaged while you focus on worship.

Practical Tips for Everyday Efficiency

BATCH COOK FOR IFTAR
Prepare meals in large quantities and
freeze them to save time for worship.

SIMPLIFY IFTAR MEALS
Keep iftar light and simple to avoid feeling sluggish. Opt for
dates, fruits, and light soups before having a balanced meal.

PLAN MEALS AHEAD
Preparing *suhoor* and *iftar* meals in advance helps
you avoid rushing and focus on nourishment and worship.

DELEGATE NON-ESSENTIAL TASKS
Share household duties with others, or delegate tasks
to create more time for worship.

DRINK WATER BETWEEN PRAYERS AT NIGHT
Stay hydrated by drinking small amounts of water between
iftar and *suhoor* to maintain energy for the next day of fasting.

MAKE THE MOST OF SUHOOR
Choose slow-releasing foods like oats and whole
grains to sustain your energy throughout the day.

PREPARE EXTRA MEALS FOR THE NEEDY
As you plan your meals, set aside portions
or organize meal prep for local families,
neighbors or even shelters.

PLAN IFTAR GATHERINGS WISELY
If hosting an iftar, consider simple meals or a potluck-style
gathering to reduce the burden of cooking. This approach
frees up more of your time and energy for worship.

Self-Care & Mindfulness Tips

USE FASTING AS A REMINDER OF THOSE IN NEED
Reflect on the struggles of the less fortunate to increase
gratitude and inspire greater acts of giving.

FOCUS ON GRATITUDE
End your day by journaling the blessings you
are grateful to Allah (SWT) for.

NAP DURING THE DAY
Take a short 15-20 minute nap after *dhuhr*
to help recharge your energy for the rest of the day.

PRACTICE SELF-CARE
Take small moments for self-care, like a quick nap or skincare
routine, to maintain your physical and emotional health.

BE GENTLE ON YOURSELF
Understand that caring for your family is a form of worship,
and don't be hard on yourself if you can't do everything.

Physical Well-Being Tips

INCORPORATE LIGHT EXERCISE AFTER IFTAR
Engage in light physical activity like walking or stretching
to aid digestion and maintain physical health.

STAY ACTIVE WITH FAMILY-FRIENDLY WORKOUTS
Involve your family in simple workouts after
suhoor or before *iftar* to keep everyone active.

ADOPT A RAMADAN WALKING CHALLENGE
Set a goal for walking a certain number of steps daily or
weekly, dedicating the physical effort to those in need.

INCORPORATE DHIKR WHILE DOING CHORES
Use everyday chores as an opportunity to make
dhikr and keep your heart spiritually connected.

AVOID TIME-WASTERS AFTER IFTAR
After breaking your fast, avoid excessive chatting, entertainment
or distractions. Instead, use that time for prayer or reflection.

Sadaqah Tips

SUPPORT LOCAL AND GLOBAL CAUSES
Donate to relief efforts providing food, water, or medical aid to communities in need, strengthening our bonds as an ummah.

SET TIME FOR CHARITY
Dedicate a specific day or time each week for giving *sadaqah*, volunteering, or helping those less fortunate.

ORGANIZE A CHARITY DRIVE
Collaborate with friends or family to collect donations for those in need, making your Ramadan impactful for others.

GIVE THROUGHOUT RAMADAN
Maximize your impact in Ramadan by setting up incremental donations. Consistent giving throughout the month not only multiplies your rewards but also ensures continuous support for those in need.

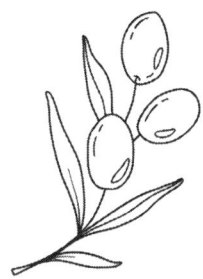

The Sunnah Food Guide

The Prophetic Diet for Health & Healing

> *"The son of Adam does not fill any vessel worse than his stomach. It is sufficient for the son of Adam to eat a few mouthfuls to keep him going. But if he must do it (i.e., eat more), then one-third for his food, one-third for his drink, and one-third for air."*
>
> —The Prophet Muhammad (SAW)
> [Ibn Majah 3349]

Ramadan is a time of spiritual renewal, but it also reminds us of the profound connection between our physical *and* spiritual well-being.

The foods we choose to consume at *suhoor* and *iftar* not only fuel our bodies but also influence our mental clarity, emotional balance, and overall vitality. In many ways, our diet during Ramadan can be seen as a form of medicine—when chosen wisely, it strengthens us, bringing us closer to our goals of worship and reflection. But when we neglect the prophetic guidance and consume what burdens our body, the very food that should nourish us becomes more like poison, draining our energy and focus.

The Prophet Muhammad (SAW) emphasized moderation and balance in all aspects of life—including what we eat. *Suhoor*, the pre-dawn meal, is described as a blessed meal, meant to sustain us through long hours of fasting. *Iftar*, the breaking of the fast, should be a moment of replenishment.

In this chapter, you will learn more about the best foods to eat at *suhoor* and *iftar*, taking inspiration from the *sunnah*. You'll also find additional information on how these foods can fuel your body, protect your energy, and make fasting easier. With this knowledge, you can add more variety to your cooking and turn your meals into a source of strength and healing.

Disclaimer: The dietary advice shared here is intended for informational purposes only. It is important to consult with a healthcare provider or a medical professional before making any significant changes to your diet. A healthcare provider can help tailor the best approach to your individual health needs and ensure that any dietary choices are appropriate for your unique circumstances.

Sunnah Foods to Eat at Suhoor (Before Fasting)

DATES
The Prophet (SAW) recommended starting the day with dates.
They are a great source of natural sugar, energy, and fiber.

WATER
Drinking plenty of water at *suhoor* is important
for hydration throughout the day.

BARLEY
The Prophet (SAW) would consume barley, often in the form of
bread or *talbinah* (a dish made with barley and milk) as a remedy
for grief and sickness. Barley is high in fiber, aiding digestion and
helping reduce cholesterol.

OATS
Oats or other whole grains are nutritious
sources of energy for the day.

MILK
The Prophet (SAW) said, *"There is nothing like milk,
which suffices both as food and drink."* [Abi Dawud 3730].
Milk is an excellent source of calcium, protein and vitamins,
benefiting bone health and overall nourishment.

HONEY
Mentioned in the Quran for its healing properties,
honey can be included as a sweetener or eaten directly.

Sunnah Foods to Eat at Iftar
(After Fasting)

DATES
The Prophet (SAW) broke his fast with dates before praying.
If no dates were available, he would use water.

WATER
Hydrating with water is essential for replenishing the body.

MILK OR BUTTERMILK
These were also part of his Iftar, offering nutrition and hydration.

SOUP OR BROTH
Lentil soup or broth made with barley was commonly eaten
by the Prophet (SAW). These options are light
and easy on the stomach.

OLIVE OIL
The Prophet (SAW) praised olive oil, saying, *"Eat olive oil and
use it on your hair and skin, for it comes from a blessed tree."*
[Tirmidhi 1852]. Olive oil is rich in healthy fats and antioxidants,
promoting heart and skin health.

VINEGAR
The Prophet (SAW) is known to have dipped bread in vinegar.
Vinegar aids digestion and helps with blood sugar control.

Other Sunnah foods

(each praised for their health benefits & nourishing qualities)

FIGS

Figs are mentioned in *Surah At-Teen* (95:1) of the Quran.
They are rich in fiber, vitamins, and minerals, promoting
digestive health and supporting overall wellness.

POMEGRANATE

The Quran (55:68) refers to pomegranates as
a fruit from paradise. Rich in antioxidants and vitamins,
pomegranates support heart health and overall vitality.

WATERMELON

The Prophet (SAW) enjoyed eating watermelon.
Watermelon is hydrating and full of vitamins A and C,
making it perfect for refreshing the body.

PUMPKIN

The Prophet (SAW) was fond of pumpkin, and
Anas ibn Malik reported seeing him search for pieces of
pumpkin in his soup [Muslim 5071]. Pumpkin is
rich in vitamins, particularly vitamin A,
which supports immune health.

CUCUMBER

The Prophet (SAW) often ate cucumber with dates.
Cucumber is hydrating and helps cool the body,
making it ideal for hot weather.

MEAT

The Prophet (SAW) enjoyed meat—especially lamb, as part of his
diet. Meat provides essential nutrients, including protein and iron,
vital for maintaining energy and strength.

BLACK SEED

The Prophet (SAW) said, "*There is healing in black seed for every disease, except death*" [Ibn Majah 3447]. Black seed is celebrated for its wide range of health benefits, including immune system support, anti-inflammatory properties, and its ability to improve respiratory health.

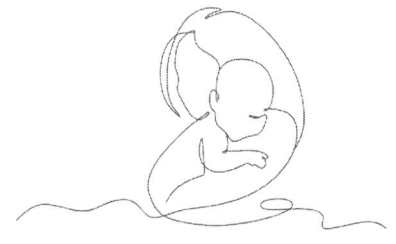

A Mama's Guide

Inspiring Your Children to Love the Blessed Month

"The best of you are those who are best to their families."

—The Prophet Muhammad (SAW)
[Tirmidhi]

Why Ramadan is a Special Time for Mothers & Children

Ramadan is such a beautiful month—especially for mothers and children. It is the perfect opportunity to create lasting memories and instill values that will shape your children's hearts forever. As a mother, *you* set the tone for how your family experiences this sacred time. Understanding this responsibility will help you accept that Ramadan is not just for you—but it is also for those you love the most.

That being said, motherhood in Ramadan can feel more challenging. During these moments especially, I want you to remember that your intentions and patience are key—especially when the days do not go as planned. There will be moments of calm and moments of chaos, and that's okay. Even on the hardest days—when nothing seems to go right—your efforts to honor Ramadan in your home have been witnessed by Allah (SWT).

Allah (SWT) reminds us in the Quran, *"Fasting is prescribed to you as it was prescribed to those before you, that you may become righteous."* (2:183). So when our children see us praying, fasting, or helping others, they naturally associate Ramadan with love, compassion, and community. Children are the greatest imitators, after all. And if you seek to instill righteousness in them, you must first begin by embodying those qualities yourself.

By making Ramadan joyful and purposeful for them, we're not just creating fond memories—we are shaping their lifelong relationship with Islam. These moments, no matter how imperfect, form the building blocks of their spiritual journey while enriching our own. When we see it through this lens, our focus naturally shifts to nurturing the torchbearers of tomorrow—our children.

Making Ramadan Fun and Interactive for Children

Building early connections with Ramadan not only encourages your child's spiritual development but also aligns with what we know about child development from a scientific perspective. Research shows that children's early experiences play a crucial role in shaping their values, behavior, and emotional attachment to traditions. The brain's plasticity during childhood means that the more exposure children have to meaningful rituals and positive associations, the more likely these practices will stick with them throughout their lives.

When our children experience Ramadan, they build emotional and cognitive connections to those memories. Studies in developmental psychology also suggest that repetitive, family-centered rituals contribute to a child's sense of identity and belonging. This means that by simply making Ramadan engaging and enjoyable for your kids, you can nurture the positive emotions and feelings they have in connection to their *deen*. These formative experiences will shape how they think about Islam *and* how they think about themselves. Building positive practices with them throughout this month will also strengthen their attachment to the family unit. This will give them a strong sense of identity and belonging to a value system greater than just themselves.

When we invite our children to participate—whether by setting the *iftar* table or trying a half-day fast—it is about so much more than the actions themselves. We're creating a loving, nurturing environment where they feel deeply connected to their faith and family. These small, meaningful moments become the foundation of their spiritual journey, shaping them into adults who cherish and value Islam.

To make Ramadan even more engaging, consider incorporating fun and interactive activities. Ramadan-themed games or scavenger hunts, for example, can make learning about fasting and charity exciting. You could design a scavenger hunt where kids search for items like a prayer mat, a Quran, or ingredients for iftar. Worksheets, puzzles, or quiet-time activities centered around Ramadan can also help children reflect while keeping them engaged.

Another idea is "Ramadan Bingo," where children mark off tasks like reading a chapter of the Quran, making *dua*, or helping someone in need. These playful activities add a sense of joy and accomplishment while reinforcing the core values of Ramadan.

Balancing Personal Spirituality and Motherhood During Ramadan

Balancing your own spirituality with the demands of motherhood during Ramadan is *not* easy. But it is so important to remember that our role as mothers—especially during this blessed month—is itself an act of worship. The Prophet (SAW) said, "The best of you are those who are best to their families" [Tirmidhi]. When we care for our children and manage our household, it is not a distraction from our spirituality—*it is part of it*. Every act of service, even if it feels mundane, is rewarded.

But that does not mean that we do not need time for ourselves. Finding moments for personal worship and reflection is still necessary for our own spiritual growth. This might look like making *istighfar* before you close your fast or taking a few minutes to make *dhikr* while the kids nap. Carving out even the smallest spaces for personal connection with Allah (SWT) will help you recharge and reconnect.

Remember, my sister, that striking a balance between fulfilling our family responsibilities and dedicating time to personal worship is a deeply rewarding act in the eyes of Allah (SWT). *Both roles carry immense value by bringing us closer to Him.*

Planting the Seeds of Love for Ramadan

Children understand Ramadan differently depending on their age, which makes it crucial to tailor explanations that are simple and relatable. For younger children, you can introduce Ramadan as a special month when we fast to please Allah (SWT) and help those in need. As they grow older, these conversations can naturally expand to include deeper concepts such as self-control, gratitude, and the rewards of fasting. By gradually deepening their understanding, you can nurture their curiosity and connection to this blessed month.

When teaching the core acts of worship in Ramadan—fasting, prayer, charity, and connecting with the Quran—it helps to weave these lessons into daily conversations and activities. One effective way to achieve this is through stories and play; this approach not only engages children but also leave a more lasting impact. Research consistently shows that interactive methods like storytelling, singing, or guided play significantly enhance children's learning compared to traditional instruction. For instance, sharing a Ramadan-themed storybook during bedtime or using hand and finger puppets to act out a fun story or song about fasting and kindness can reinforce lessons in a much more powerful way for children. Whichever approach you choose with your children, ensure it is encouraging and loving. This will help foster a positive connection between faith and joy in their hearts.

Creating a Ramadan Atmosphere in Your Home

One of the best ways to make Ramadan special for children is by creating a festive and spiritual atmosphere at home. For example, decorating together can make the experience exciting for little children. Engaging them in DIY crafts, like making banners, lanterns, or crescent moon decorations, not only keeps them away from screens but can also be a bonding exercise with them when doing these activities together. These crafts can also be a great way to passively educate your children on the importance of the symbols of Ramadan, such as the crescent moon that marks its beginning and end.

Another way to build excitement is by creating a special Ramadan corner at home. This cozy space, equipped with prayer mats, and Islamic books will allow your children to take ownership of their spiritual journey. It gives them a dedicated area to engage with Ramadan in a way that feels special for them. These small touches not only create memorable experiences but also preserve the beauty and uniqueness of our traditions.

While it is wonderful to make Ramadan fun and memorable, it is equally important to honor its unique identity as an Islamic tradition. The Prophet Muhammad (SAW) emphasized the importance of preserving our distinct identity as Muslims. He specifically mentioned that as Muslims, we are to celebrate only two festivals: Eid ul-Fitr and Eid ul-Adha. In a narration, Anas ibn Malik (RA) reported that when the Prophet (SAW) came to Madinah, he observed people celebrating two days. He asked about them, and they replied that these were days of fun from the pre-Islamic era. The Prophet (SAW) then said:

"Allah has replaced these two days with something better: the day of al-Adha and the day of al-Fitr."

—The Prophet Muhammad (SAW)
[An-Nasa'i 1556]

This statement reinforces the idea that as Muslims, we should be focusing our attention on the days that Allah (SWT) has gifted us, without feeling the need to imitate other faiths and traditions. *We should be proud of our religion.* Additionally, the Prophet (SAW) warned against imitating other faiths, saying:

"Whoever imitates a people is one of them."

—The Prophet Muhammad (SAW)
[Abu Dawood 4031]

Rather than letting our children be drawn to the allure of other holidays, it is our responsibility to create a joyful and meaningful atmosphere around our own celebrations. This helps instill pride in their Islamic identity and a deep love for their faith.

As Muslims living in the West, this can feel like a challenge. Holidays like Halloween and Christmas, with their candy, decorations, and bright lights, can seem hard to compete with. But we must remember that Islam is the truth, and that is our greatest strength. By making Ramadan and our two Eids vibrant, engaging, and filled with meaning, we give our children a sense of belonging and joy in their own traditions. This way, they won't feel they're "missing out" but instead will cherish the beauty and richness of their faith.

Involve Your Children in Acts of Worship

Prayer is the heart of our connection to Allah (SWT), and Ramadan is the wonderful time to nurture this love for *salah* in our children.

Organizing family prayer times during Ramadan can turn *salah* into something your children look forward to. You can create a fun, interactive prayer chart where each family member gets to mark off their completed prayers, and perhaps even compete in a reward system. This can help to build a sense of accomplishment and makes them feel included in the family's spiritual journey.

Also, you can encourage your children to join *taraweeh* with you at home or at the masjid. Even if your child only joins for a few short *rakah*, this gives them a glimpse of the beauty of night prayers. Keep it light and joyful, maybe even inviting them to wear their favorite prayer outfits or setting up comfortable mats and dim lighting.

Fasting for Little Ones

Fasting is one of the core pillars of Ramadan, and while younger children are not required to fast, we can still introduce them to the idea in a gentle and age-appropriate way. One popular approach is "half-day" fasts, where kids fast until noon or a specific time. This lets them feel involved without overwhelming them. The focus is not on the obligation but on teaching them the spirit of fasting—helping them associate it with patience, gratitude, and empathy.

The Prophet Muhammad (SAW) beautifully said, *"The one who fasts has two joys: one when he breaks his fast, and the other when he meets his Lord"* [Muslim 1151d]. By allowing children to experience even a small part of fasting, they can share in the joy and feel a sense of accomplishment.

Another way to involve them is through *suhoor* and *iftar* preparations. Let them help with simple tasks—choosing dates for iftar, setting the table, or arranging plates. These little moments build their self-esteem and allow them to feel connected with Ramadan.

Incorporating Dua and Dhikr

Teaching children the power of *dua* and *dhikr* in Ramadan is another beautiful way to involve them in acts of worship. Simple *dua'*, such as the one for beginning the fast—*"I intend to keep the fast for tomorrow in the month of Ramadan"*—and the one for breaking it—*"O Allah, I have fasted for You, I believe in You, and with Your sustenance, I break my fast"*—are excellent for children to learn. These small acts of worship are a great way to engage them and remind them that Ramadan is not just about fasting but also about connecting with Allah (SWT) through our *dua*.

Encouraging Charity and Kindness

An effective way to teach our children about the value of giving is by engaging them in small acts of charity. Some examples of this are by donating toys or clothing to those in need or helping to prepare meals for less fortunate families. This is also a reminder for us that acts of service to others are a manifestation of our belief in Allah (SWT).

Another activity that can be done to reinforce this message to your children is creating a "Kindness Jar." Each day, family members can write down a good deed they'd like to accomplish and put it in the jar. At the end of the day, everyone can pick one deed to do together, whether it is helping a neighbor or volunteering at a local charity. This activity not only reinforces the importance of kindness but also makes it an interactive experience for the whole family.

Accept Being Imperfectly Perfect

Motherhood in Ramadan is a journey, and like any journey, it comes with its share of twists and turns. Some days will feel smooth— you'll find yourself managing *suhoor*, prayers, fasting, and even creating special moments with your children with ease. Other days, you might feel like you're barely holding it together, struggling to balance your *ibadah* with the endless demands of parenting. And that's okay. This is the nature of motherhood: it's unpredictable, messy, and beautifully imperfect.

Patience will be your greatest ally throughout this month. When the day doesn't go as planned—when your toddler spills juice during *iftar* prep, or the baby wakes up crying just as you're about to pray—remind yourself that even in these moments, you're worshiping Allah (SWT). Caring for your family, showing patience, and choosing kindness over frustration are all acts of *ibadah*—especially during Ramadan.

It's also important to forgive yourself on the "hard" days. Maybe you couldn't finish the extra Quran reading you'd planned, or you ended up breaking your fast while rocking a fussy baby to sleep instead of at the *iftar* table. These moments don't diminish the sincerity of your efforts. Allah (SWT) sees the sacrifices you make and the love you pour into your family, even when you feel stretched thin.

Motherhood in Ramadan isn't about perfection—it's about intention. Every *dua* you whisper while washing dishes, every effort you make to teach your children about the beauty of this month, and every time you choose patience over anger, you're building something meaningful. So, take it one day at a time, knowing that Allah (SWT) rewards both your visible acts of worship and the unseen struggles that only He knows.

Navigating Your Cycle

Practical Tips for Menstruation
During Ramadan to Optimize
Worship & Spiritual Growth

> *"Whoever does righteousness, whether male or female,*
> *while they are a believer–We will surely cause them to live a good*
> *life, and We will surely give them their reward [in the Hereafter]*
> *according to the best of what they used to do."*
>
> —The Quran (16:97)

As we welcome the holy month of Ramadan, it's essential to address a topic that often feels taboo but is completely natural: menstruation. Otherwise known as: *getting your period.*

Many of us have grown up with mixed messages about our cycles, leading to a sense of shame or discomfort in discussing this important aspect of being a woman. However, menstruation is nothing to be ashamed of; it's a gift from Allah (SWT) and a beautiful reflection of our ability to bear children. It's simply part of the experience of womanhood.

The women around the Messenger of Allah (SAW) were confident and assertive about their questions regarding menstruation. One notable hadith tells of a woman who approached the Prophet (SAW) asking about a specific issue related to her menstrual cycle. This openness among the companions shows that it's not only acceptable to talk about menstruation but also encouraged. In fact, seeking knowledge about our bodies and experiences is an important part of our faith.

In this chapter, we are going to talk about *why* it is so important to address menstruation during Ramadan. It's something many of us do not always have safe spaces to discuss, but it is such an essential part of our experience during this month. You will also find tips on how to stay spiritually connected, even when you cannot fast or pray, and advice on what to eat for *suhoor* and *iftar* to keep your energy up.

But Ramadan is not just about what we do physically—it's also about taking care of ourselves and our community of muslimah's. Sharing our experiences and leaning on one another can make a big difference in feeling comfortable and supported. So, let's begin.

Understanding Menstruation in Islam

Menstruation is a natural part of a woman's life, and in Islam, it is treated with understanding and respect—despite what you may have been told. Allah (SWT) recognizes the physical and emotional experiences we as women go through during this time and has given us guidance in the Quran and Hadith to help us navigate it with grace and mindfulness.

The Prophet Muhammad (SAW) showed us how to handle menstruation with kindness and understanding. Aisha (RA) shared that women would often ask the Prophet (SAW) about what they could or could not do during their cycles, and he always responded with clarity and compassion. One woman even asked the Prophet (SAW) about fasting during her period, and he gently advised her on how to make up the fasts afterward. This shows that menstruation should be approached openly—without shame or discomfort.

It is important to note here that while we are excused from fasting and prayer during this time, we are *still* encouraged to stay connected to Allah (SWT) through *dhikr*, *dua*, giving charity, and more. Islam teaches us that menstruation is not a time of spiritual loss. In fact, it can be an opportunity for self-care, reflection, and a reminder of the natural processes Allah (SWT) has created.

Ritual Purity (Taharah)

In Islam, *taharah*, or ritual purity, is a core element of worship. It represents the state of cleanliness required for performing acts of devotion, such as prayer and fasting. During menstruation, women are temporarily exempt from obligations like *salah* and fasting because they are not in a state of *taharah*. However, this does not diminish our value or spiritual worth. In fact, this time opens the door for us to engage in other forms of worship, like making *dua*, reciting *dhikr*, or reflecting on the Quran. By reframing menstruation as a natural part of life that temporarily shifts our worship practices, we can embrace this time with grace, free from guilt or shame.

Debunking Common Myths About Menstruation in Islam

Despite the clear guidance from Allah (SWT), many misconceptions about menstruation still exist. One common myth is that menstruating women are considered "unclean" or unworthy of engaging in *any* form of worship. This belief is not supported by Islamic teachings. In reality, menstruation is a natural process, part of Allah's (SWT) divine design, and should never be a source of shame. It reflects the incredible ability of women to create life, and this should be honored—not hidden.

I remember growing up and talking to Muslim friends at school who would wake up early to eat *suhoor*, pretending to fast just to avoid questions from male family members. There was a sense of shame around menstruation that made them feel the need to hide it. Sadly, this behavior often comes from cultural norms that overshadow the true teachings of Islam. Rather than feeling comfortable talking about our cycles, many women are left to navigate this sacred month in silence, fearing judgment or misunderstanding.

In many cultures, menstruation is still stigmatized, which can create unhealthy associations with our bodies and limit open conversations. It is important to distinguish between cultural practices and the teachings of Islam. While certain traditions may unintentionally perpetuate shame, Islam encourages understanding, acceptance, and open dialogue about menstruation.

Another misconception is that menstruating women cannot engage in any religious activities at all. While it is true that acts like *salah* and fasting are not obligatory during this time, women can still actively participate in many spiritual practices, such as reciting Quran (so long as they are not physically touching the *mus'haf*), making *dua*, and performing acts of charity. *Remember, menstruation does not diminish your connection with Allah (SWT).*

Understanding Your Menstrual Cycle

Understanding your menstrual cycle is an essential part of knowing your body and taking care of your health. Many women overlook the importance of tracking their cycles and learning how the different phases can affect their energy, mood, and well-being—knowledge that can be particularly beneficial during the fasting month.

Phases of the Menstrual Cycle

The menstrual cycle is divided into four main phases, each with its own physiological effects. These phases are not only important in relation to reproductive health but also affect how we feel physically and emotionally. Here's an overview of the key phases:

MENSTRUAL PHASE

This is the phase we're most familiar with—it's the time of active bleeding. During this phase, your body sheds the lining of the uterus, and you may feel low energy, experience cramping, and have cravings. This is also the phase when fasting is not obligatory.

focus on: Rest and replenishment.

FOLLICULAR PHASE

The follicular phase begins right after menstruation and lasts until ovulation. This phase is marked by rising estrogen levels, and many women notice increased energy and focus. It's a great time for mental clarity and productivity.

focus on: Planning worship or other activities.

OVULATORY PHASE

Ovulation is when one of your ovaries releases an egg, typically around the middle of your cycle. Energy levels are often at their peak during this phase.

focus on: Maximizing your worship or community involvement during Ramadan, as you'll likely feel more energetic and positive.

LUTEAL PHASE

After ovulation, the body enters the luteal phase, when progesterone levels rise. Some women experience PMS (premenstrual syndrome) during this time, including bloating, mood swings, or irritability. You may find yourself more tired or craving comfort foods.

focus on: Be kind to yourself, and those around you. Your body may need more rest or nourishing food during this time.

Worship During Menstruation

Menstruation may temporarily exempt us from certain acts of worship. However, there are many other beautiful ways to remain spiritually connected and express our devotion to Allah (SWT).

Permissible Acts of Worship

1. ENGAGING IN DHIKR (REMEMBRANCE OF ALLAH)

One of the most profound ways to stay connected with Allah (SWT) is through *dhikr*. This can include reciting phrases like *SubhanAllah* (Glory be to Allah), *Alhamdulillah* (Praise be to Allah), and *Allahu Akbar* (Allah is the Greatest). Engaging in dhikr can bring peace to the heart and keep our minds focused on the blessings and mercy of Allah (SWT). Ensure that you are also completing your morning and evening *adhkar* too.

2. MAKING DUA (SUPPLICATION) AND SEEKING FORGIVENESS

During menstruation, we can still communicate with Allah (SWT) through *dua*. This intimate form of worship allows us to ask for guidance, healing, and strength. It is also a time to seek forgiveness for any shortcomings and reflect on our relationship with Allah (SWT).

3. READING AND RECITING THE QURAN (WITHOUT PHYSICAL CONTACT)

While it's not permissible to touch the physical Arabic Quran (the *mus'haf*) during menstruation, we can still read and recite the Quran using a translation or by memorization. In recent years, some scholars have shared that using a digital version of the Quran on our phones or tablets is permissible, as it's not considered the same as the physical *mus'haf* (the written copy of the Quran). This means that if you have a Quran app on your phone, you can still engage with the Quran during your cycle. It can actually be a great opportunity to focus on understanding the meanings of the Quran and reflecting on how they apply to your personal life.

4. ACTS OF CHARITY AND COMMUNITY SERVICE

Engaging in acts of charity is another meaningful way to worship during menstruation. In Islam, charity is highly valued and considered an act of worship. This could look like helping a neighbor, donating to a cause, or volunteering; these actions not only benefit others but also bring spiritual rewards.

Understanding Fidyah

Fidyah is a form of compensation in Islam for those who are unable to fast during Ramadan due to valid reasons—including menstruation. Understanding the rulings surrounding *fidyah* can help clarify its purpose and how to fulfill this obligation appropriately.

Who is required to pay fidyah?

Fidyah is applicable to those who are unable to make up their missed fasts before the next Ramadan. This includes individuals who may have chronic illnesses, severe health conditions, or women who cannot fast due to menstruation. If you have your menstrual cycle during Ramadan, you are not required to pay *fidyah* for those days. You only need to make up the same number of missed fasts at a later time.

How much is fidyah?

The amount of *fidyah* is typically determined based on the local cost of feeding a needy person. Scholars generally recommend providing enough food to feed one person for each missed day of fasting. The exact amount can vary depending on local food prices, but it is often calculated as the equivalent of a specific weight of staple food (such as wheat, dates, or barley). A common practice is to offer a meal equivalent to approximately 1.5 kg (3.3 pounds) of food.

When should fidyah be given?

Fidyah should ideally be paid when one realizes that they will not be able to make up their missed fasts before the next Ramadan. It is advisable to give *fidyah* before the next Ramadan arrives, ensuring that the compensation reaches those in need promptly. This timing reflects the importance of fulfilling our obligations and ensuring that the needy benefit from our charitable actions.

Where to give fidyah?

Fidyah can be given directly to the needy individuals in your community or through charitable organizations that distribute food to those in need. Some people choose to give *fidyah* in the form of cash to organizations that provide meals for those who are less fortunate.

Nutritional Needs During Ramadan

Taking care of our bodies is a form of worship in itself, especially during Ramadan, when our routines shift and our physical needs change. As women, menstruation adds an additional layer of consideration to the way we approach our nutrition during this sacred month. Understanding how to nourish ourselves properly is key to maintaining our health and energy, especially when we're fasting or recovering from our menstrual cycles.

Scientific Evidence on Fasting and Menstruation

Fasting while menstruating (including intermittent fasting), can negatively affect a woman's health. During menstruation, the body loses essential nutrients, especially iron, leading to fatigue or weakness. Scientific studies have shown that fasting during this time can have a range of negative effects:

1. HORMONAL IMBALANCE

Fasting can disrupt hormonal balance, particularly affecting estrogen and progesterone levels. A study published in the *Journal of the Endocrine Society* found that calorie restriction and fasting impair the hypothalamic-pituitary-gonadal (HPG) axis, which is crucial for regulating reproductive hormones. This can lead to irregular cycles and even worsen menstrual pain.

2. METABOLIC IMPACT AND FATIGUE

Fasting slows down metabolism and can increase fatigue, making it harder for women to recover during their menstrual cycle. A review in *Obesity Reviews* noted that women are more sensitive to changes in energy intake, and fasting can lead to hypoglycemia, which explains why many women feel weak, dizzy, or irritable when they attempt to fast during menstruation.

3. NUTRIENT DEFICIENCY

A study in the *American Journal of Clinical Nutrition* found that women who fasted while menstruating were more likely to experience deficiencies in essential nutrients like iron, calcium, and magnesium. These are critical for energy production, muscle function, and overall health during the menstrual cycle.

Nutritional Foods to Eat During the Day

When planning meals during Ramadan, particularly when you are menstruating, it is important to choose foods that will nourish you and keep you energized. Some nutrients play a special role in recovery and overall well-being, especially during this time.

IRON-RICH FOODS

Menstruation often depletes iron stores, which can lead to fatigue and weakness. Incorporating iron-rich foods into your diet can help replenish these levels. Foods like spinach, lentils, red meat, and beans are excellent sources of iron. Pairing them with Vitamin C-rich foods, like citrus fruits, strawberries, or bell peppers, can also enhance iron absorption.

VITAMIN AND MINERAL SOURCES

In addition to iron, it is essential to focus on foods packed with vitamins and minerals. Fruits, nuts, seeds, and vegetables are key sources of these nutrients. Dates, (a traditional *suhoor* and *iftar* staple) are packed with energy, fiber, and essential minerals like potassium and magnesium. Nuts and seeds, like almonds and chia seeds, are great for providing sustained energy, healthy fats, and antioxidants, which are helpful for overall health and recovery.

HYDRATION

Menstruation can exacerbate dehydration, so it is crucial to drink plenty of water when you are able to. If plain water feels monotonous, herbal teas, coconut water, or water-rich foods like cucumbers and watermelon can help maintain hydration and provide added nutrients.

SUSTAINING ENERGY

To keep your energy steady, focus on complex carbohydrates like whole grains, oats, and legumes. These foods provide a slow release of energy, helping you stay fuller for longer. Protein is also essential for sustained energy, so incorporating sources like eggs, yogurt, or lentils will help you feel more balanced throughout the day.

As we conclude this chapter, it is important to take a moment to reflect on the key insights we've explored. Menstruation during Ramadan is not something to feel burdened by or disconnected from—it's simply a different pace in our spiritual journey. Islam, with its beauty and wisdom, provides us with countless ways to worship and stay close to Allah (SWT), even when we cannot fast or pray. Whether through *dhikr*, *dua*, acts of charity, or service, there are endless opportunities for us to engage spiritually and make the most of this blessed month.

Seeking Laylatul Qadr

Prepare for The Night of Power, a Night Greater Than a Thousand Months

> *"Indeed, We sent the Quran down during the Night of Decree. And what will make you understand what the Night of Decree is? The Night of Decree is better than a thousand months. The angels and the Spirit (Jibreel) descend in it by the permission of their Lord with every matter. It is peace until the break of dawn."*
>
> —The Quran (97:1-5)

What is Laylatul Qadr?

Laylatul Qadr is often translated as the "Night of Decree" or the "Night of Power." It is one of the holiest and most spiritually significant nights in the Islamic year. This is the night on which the Quran was first revealed to the Prophet Muhammad (SAW), making it a pivotal moment in our Islamic history.

Allah (SWT) describes *Laylatul Qadr* in the Quran as a night that is "…better than a thousand months." (97:3), meaning that worship and good deeds performed on this night carry the reward of more than 83 years of devotion.

Numerous Hadith also emphasize its importance. The Prophet (SAW) said, *"Whoever stands (in prayer) during Laylatul Qadr out of faith and seeking reward, will have all their past sins forgiven."* [Tirmidhi 683]. From this, we understand that *Laylatul qadr* is not a night to be missed. It is the perfect opportunity for us to seek forgiveness from Allah (SWT).

This auspicious night of *Laylatul Qadr* falls within the last ten nights of Ramadan—on an odd-numbered night. No one knows exactly when it will occur—and some scholars speculate that the night changes every year. Ultimately, only Allah (SWT) knows when this night falls in Ramadan, which means that we must do our utmost to strive on *all* of the nights to ensure we catch it. Perhaps this is one of the wisdoms behind Allah (SWT) not specifying the exact night of *Laylatul qadr.*

Another virtue of this powerful night is that Allah (SWT) decrees the events of the next year for all His creation. It is written who will live and who will pass away, who will face trials and who will find ease, who will be honored and who will be humbled. It includes matters of sustenance, health, and even natural events like drought or abundance.

This is a reminder of Allah's (SWT) sovereignty and the importance of seeking His mercy and guidance during these nights. Knowing that our destinies are being decreed should inspire us to fill our nights with worship, *dua*, and seeking forgiveness.

Laylatul Qadr is not a night to feel burdened but to feel hopeful—Allah (SWT) has blessed us with an opportunity to shape our destiny through sincere acts of worship. *It is a gift.*

Personalizing Laylatul Qadr for You

Laylatul Qadr is the culmination of everything Ramadan has been building towards. Throughout this blessed month, you have been fasting, praying, and trying to strengthen your connection with Allah (SWT). This night, better than a thousand months, is where all that hard work comes together.

This night is for *you*. It is for the moments of prayer when your heart feels heavy. For the sacrifices you make to fast even when it is hard. For the days and nights when you struggle to balance worship and taking care of your family. This is what Ramadan has been leading you to—a night that could change your life *forever*.

What are the Signs of Laylatul Qadr?

According to the teachings of the Prophet Muhammad (SAW), *Laylatul Qadr* is often characterized by certain signs. One Hadith describes the atmosphere during this night as serene and tranquil—an air of peace can be tangibly felt. It is also said that the temperature may be mild, neither too hot nor too cold.

The Prophet (SAW) emphasized that *Laylatul Qadr* occurs within the last ten nights of Ramadan, particularly on the odd-numbered nights: the 21st, 23rd, 25th, 27th, and 29th. In a Hadith narrated by Abu Hurairah, he stated:

> *"Seek Laylatul Qadr in the odd-numbered nights of the last ten nights of Ramadan."*
>
> —The Prophet Muhammad (SAW)
> [Bukhari]

While many scholars believe that the 27th night is the most likely candidate for Laylatul Qadr, it is important to remain diligent and spiritually engaged throughout *all* ten nights.

We also know that certain signs may be observed the morning after *Laylatul Qadr:*

> *"On the morning after Laylatul Qadr, the sun rises without a ray (its light is weak) until it is completely risen."*
>
> [Muslim]

Practical Tips for Engaging in Worship

Here are some practical tips and acts of worship to focus on—especially in the all-important last ten nights of Ramadan:

SET YOUR INTENTIONS

Before the night begins, take a moment to set clear intentions for your worship. Remind yourself of the significance of *Laylatul Qadr* and the blessings it holds.

CREATE A CONDUCIVE ENVIRONMENT

Prepare a quiet, comfortable space for your worship, free from distractions (yes, turn your phone off). This can help you focus better on your prayers and supplications.

SHORT BURSTS OF WORSHIP

If you find it challenging to commit to long periods of worship, break it down into shorter bursts. Even ten minutes of sincere *dhikr* or recitation from the Quran can be impactful.

ENGAGE FAMILY

Involve your family in worship activities, making it a collective effort. You can all motivate one another throughout the night.

TAKE PRODUCTIVE BREAKS

During your "down time" you can listen to Islamic lectures and have a little snack. Little "pick-me-ups" like this can help keep you engaged, especially during longer sessions throughout the night.

PRIORITIZE YOUR ENERGY

Recognize your energy levels and plan your worship accordingly. If you know that you tend to feel tired later in the night, consider taking a short nap during the day to recharge. This will help you stay alert during your nighttime prayers and supplications.

Acts of Worship to Focus On

DHIKR (REMEMBRANCE OF ALLAH)

Remind yourself of Allah's (SWT) greatness by engaging in *dhikr* throughout the night, helping to keep your heart calm and focused.

RECITATION OF THE QURAN

Spend time reading and reflecting on the Quran. *Laylatul Qadr* was the night on which the Quran was revealed—just imagine the rewards of reciting the words of the Quran on this night.

DUA'

Refer back to your personalized *dua'* list (included in this journal) and remember to ask Allah (SWT) for forgiveness, guidance, and anything else you desire. (See below for more details on specific *dua'* you can make on this night). Remember that *Laylatul Qadr* is a time when prayers are more likely to be accepted.

ISTIGHFAR (SEEKING FORGIVENESS)

Seek forgiveness sincerely for past mistakes and shortcomings. The Prophet (SAW) taught us that Allah (SWT) loves those who turn to Him in repentance.

EXTRA PRAYERS (TAHAJJUD, QIYAM AL-LAYL)

Pray *taraweeh*, and additional rakah throughout the night. Then pray *tahajjud* in the last third of the night. Make sure you dedicate specific time to asking for forgiveness before *suhoor* time comes in.

ACTS OF CHARITY

Set aside a specific amount of charity to give during the last ten nights of Ramadan. Divide this total into ten portions and donate one portion each night. This way, you maximize your chances of giving on Laylatul Qadr.

Special Dua for Laylatul Qadr

The Prophet Muhammad (SAW) taught us that
the most powerful *dua* that can be recited
specifically on this blessed night is:

اللَّهُمَّ إِنَّكَ عَفُوٌّ تُحِبُّ الْعَفْوَ فَاعْفُ عَنِّي

Allahumma innaka 'afuwwun tuhibbu al-'afwa fa'fu 'anni

Oh Allah, You are Pardoning and
You love to pardon, so pardon me.

By reciting this *dua*, we acknowledge our shortcomings and ask Allah (SWT) to erase our sins.

Ultimately, Laylatul Qadr is a reminder that Allah's (SWT) mercy is vast and that every effort made during these nights is witnessed by Him. Remember that this time is more so about quality—not quantity. This means that in order to receive the most reward, your heart must be present with every act of worship you engage in. Every prayer. Every word you recite from the Quran. Every *dua* you make—be mindful, and engage your heart in it.

As you step into these last ten nights of Ramadan, may you find peace, clarity, and an abundance of blessings. May your heart be filled with gratitude and contentment, and may Allah (SWT) grant you and your family the best of this world, and the best of the *akhirah. Ameen.*

Eid Al-Fitr

A Guide to Celebrating Eid, the Sunnah Way

"When the Day of Eid comes, wear your best clothes, for it is a day of celebration."

—The Prophet Muhammad (SAW)
[Ibn Majah]

Say This Greeting to Others on Eid Day

تقبل الله منا ومنكم

Taqabbal Allahu minna wa minkum

May Allah accept [good deeds]
from us and from you.

You made it. A whole month of intense worship and sacrifice—now you can enjoy the festivities of Eid. May Allah (SWT) accept all of our worship in the month of Ramadan, Ameen!

As you approach Eid ul-Fitr, there are no strict rules on how to celebrate, and each culture brings its own unique traditions to the occasion. However, the Prophet Muhammad (SAW) provided us with valuable guidance on how to observe this blessed day. Below, you'll find details on how to make the most of this special occasion—the *sunnah* way.

1. MAKE GHUSL BEFORE THE EID PRAYER

*"The messenger of Allah used to have
a bath on the day of Fitr."*

[Ibn Majah]

2. DRESSING IN NEW OR BEST CLOTHES

*"When the Day of Eid comes, wear your best clothes,
for it is a day of celebration."*

—The Prophet Muhammad (SAW)
[Ibn Majah]

This hadith emphasizes that Eid is a day of festivity and happiness, and it is recommended to dress in your finest clothes to honor the significance of the occasion.

3. WEAR PERFUME *(for men only)*

"The Prophet (SAW) used to wear the best of his clothes and apply perfume on the day of Eid."

[Ibn Majah]

4. EAT SOMETHING BEFORE THE EID SALAH

"The Prophet (SAW) would eat on the morning of Eid ul-Fitr before going to the prayer, but he would not eat on the morning of Eid al-Adha until after he had offered the prayer and slaughtered the sacrifice."

[Ibn Majah]

This hadith shows the practice of eating a small meal before attending the Eid ul-Fitr prayer, which is a recommended *sunnah*. The meal is often something light, such as dates (an odd-numbered amount), as demonstrated by the Prophet (SAW).

5. SAY TAKBEER

Takbeeraat for Eid are to be recited in the following manner:

"Allahu Akbar, Allahu Akbar, Allahu Akbar, La ilaha illallah, Allahu Akbar, Allahu Akbar, wa lillahi al-hamd."

This is typically said from the *maghrib* prayer of the night before Eid until the Eid prayer itself.

6. THE ROUTE TO EID SALAH

*"On the Day of Eid, the Prophet (SAW) would take
one route to the prayer ground and return by another."*

[Bukhari]

7. PAY ZAKATUL FITR BEFORE THE SALAH

*"The Sadaqat-ul-Fitr should be paid
before the people go out for prayer."*

—The Prophet Muhammad (SAW)
[Muslim 986a]

Zakatul Fitr is an obligatory act of charity before the Eid *salah* to purify the fast. This hadith emphasizes the importance of paying *Zakatul Fitr* before performing the Eid prayer to ensure the acceptance of one's fast and to help those in need.

8. PRAYING EID PRAYER

*"The Messenger of Allah (SAW) commanded us to bring out the
women and young girls on the two Eids, so they could witness
the goodness and the gathering of the Muslims. But he told the
menstruating women to keep away from the place where the
people pray."*

[An-Nasa'i 1559]

9. CONGRATULATE EACH OTHER

Greet others with the statement, *"Taqabbal Allahu minna wa min-kum,"* meaning, "May Allah accept [good deeds] from us and from you."

10. GIVE GIFTS

"Give gifts, for they increase love between you."

—The Prophet Muhammad (SAW)
[Bukhari]

Giving gifts on Eid as an act of kindness that strengthens bonds of affection and unity among Muslims. It's a way to show love and appreciation to one another, making Eid even more special.

11. ENJOY THE DAY!

*"The day of Eid ul-Fitr is a day of festivity,
and the day of Eid ul-Adha is a day of sacrifice."*

—The Prophet Muhammad (SAW)
[Bukhari]

Eid ul-Fitr is a day of joy and celebration after a month of fasting. This hadith reminds us that Eid is a time to enjoy the blessings of Allah (SWT), spend time with family, and partake in the festive atmosphere.

May this Eid be filled with peace, love, and an abundance of blessings for you and your family. As you celebrate, remember to carry the spirit of gratitude, reflection, and kindness with you. Eid Mubarak!

My Gift List

Create a List of Thoughtful Gifts for Your Loved Ones

> *"Exchange gifts,*
> *and you will love one another."*
>
> —The Prophet Muhammad (SAW)
> [Bukhari]

Use this section to list the family and loved ones you'd like to give gifts to this Eid. Remember, a gift is about the thought and care behind it, not its size or cost. It's a way to show love, appreciation, and thoughtfulness to the special people in your life. Take a moment to write down what gift you'd like to give each person—whether it's something handmade, a heartfelt note, or a token of gratitude. Let this be a joyful part of your Eid preparation, focusing on the connection and intention behind each gesture.

I want to give a gift to...	*The gift will be...*

I want to give a gift to…	*The gift will be…*

I want to give a gift to…	*The gift will be…*

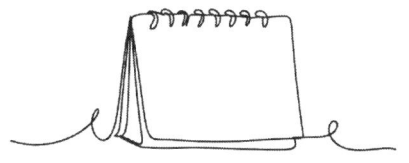

My Daily Planner

Meticulously Plan Each Day of Ramadan With Intention— from your Salaah to Your Meals & Beyond

This section is designed to help you plan and organize each day of Ramadan with ease. Each page is dedicated to an individual day, like "Day 1, Day 2," and so on, so you can map out your schedule thoughtfully. You'll find space to plan your suhoor and iftar meals, track your salaah progress, and set intentions for the day. A mindfulness section is also included, encouraging you to reflect and recenter yourself both at the start and end of each day. This will help you approach the next with clarity and purpose.

RAMADAN AT A GLANCE

Use this monthly planner to effortlessly track key dates, daily themes, and important events throughout Ramadan. This will help you stay on top of your worship and stay organized in other areas by visualizing the month ahead.

monday	tuesday	wednesday	thursday	friday	saturday	sunday

DAY 1
ramadan

"When the month of Ramadan starts, the gates
of the heaven are opened and the gates of Hell
are closed and the devils are chained."

—The Prophet Muhammad (SAW)
[Bukhari 1899]

Thoughts I choose to release as I begin today...

Take a moment to jot down everything on your mind—tasks, worries, grudges, anything at all. This quick exercise will help you begin your day with a clear heart & mind.

ramadan
DAY 1

my schedule

12 AM

1 AM

2 AM

3 AM

4 AM

5 AM

6 AM

7 AM

8 AM

9 AM

10 AM

11 AM

12 PM

1 PM

2 PM

3 PM

4 PM

5 PM

6 PM

7 PM

8 PM

9 PM

10 PM

11 PM

are you fasting today?

○ YES   ○ NO, I'M EXCUSED

DID YOU PAY YOUR FIDYAH? Y / N

suhoor ☼

iftar ☾

workout

○ YES   ○ NO

💡 did you know...

Studies show that fasting can boost brain function by improving memory and focus.

daily Quran:

	JUZZ	CHAPTER	VERSE
START:			
FINISH:			

good deeds:

○ I GAVE IN CHARITY   ○ I VISITED A SICK PERSON
○ I HELPED SOMEONE IN NEED   ○ I DID A SECRET GOOD DEED
○ I FORGAVE SOMEONE   ○ I SPOKE WITH MY PARENTS
○ I FED A HUNGRY PERSON   ○ I HOSTED IFTAR

prayers

○ FAJR   ○ ISHA
○ DHUR   ○ TARAWEEH
○ ASR   ○ TAHAJJUD
○ MAGHRIB

adhkaar

○ MORNING
○ EVENING

additional notes

fill this section out at the end of each day

A moment for
Mindfulness

Now let's check-in with how you're feeling spiritually and emotionally...

I am feeling...

😠 😫 🙁 🙂 😆
ANGRY　TIRED　SAD　HAPPY　EXCITED

I feel this way right now because...

Alhamdulillah for...

Have I taken a moment to pause, breathe, and reconnect with my intentions today?

Y / N

What spiritual lesson(s) did I learn today?

Which of Allah's names or attributes did you feel most connected to today? Why?

Did you let go of anything today that was weighing on your heart?

Something I will do for self-care tomorrow is...

To be a better version of myself tomorrow, inshaAllah I will...

additional notes

DAY 2
ramadan

"The (reward of) deeds, depend upon the
intentions and every person will get the reward
according to what he has intended. So whoever
emigrated for the sake of Allah and His Apostle,
then his emigration will be considered to be for
Allah and His Apostle, and whoever emigrated
for the sake of worldly gain or for a woman to
marry, then his emigration will be considered
to be for what he emigrated for."

—The Prophet Muhammad (pbuh)
[Bukhari 6689]

Thoughts I choose to release as I begin today...

Take a moment to jot down everything on your mind—tasks, worries, grudges, anything at all. This quick exercise will help you begin your day with a clear heart & mind.

ramadan
DAY 2

my schedule

12 AM

1 AM

2 AM

3 AM

4 AM

5 AM

6 AM

7 AM

8 AM

9 AM

10 AM

11 AM

12 PM

1 PM

2 PM

3 PM

4 PM

5 PM

6 PM

7 PM

8 PM

9 PM

10 PM

11 PM

---

are you fasting today?

○ YES   ○ NO, I'M EXCUSED

DID YOU PAY YOUR FIDYAH? Y / N

suhoor ☀

iftar ☾

workout

○ YES   ○ NO

did you know...

During fasting, your body removes damaged cells and makes room for new, healthier ones, a process called autophagy.

daily Quran:

	JUZZ	CHAPTER	VERSE
START:			
FINISH:			

good deeds:

○ I GAVE IN CHARITY   ○ I VISITED A SICK PERSON

○ I HELPED SOMEONE IN NEED   ○ I DID A SECRET GOOD DEED

○ I FORGAVE SOMEONE   ○ I SPOKE WITH MY PARENTS

○ I FED A HUNGRY PERSON   ○ I HOSTED IFTAR

prayers

○ FAJR   ○ ISHA

○ DHUR   ○ TARAWEEH

○ ASR   ○ TAHAJJUD

○ MAGHRIB

adhkaar

○ MORNING

○ EVENING

additional notes

fill this section
out at the end
of each day

A moment for
Mindfulness

Now let's check-in with how you're feeling spiritually and emotionally...

I am feeling...

ANGRY   TIRED   SAD   HAPPY   EXCITED

I feel this way right now because...

Alhamdulillah for...

Have I taken a moment to pause, breathe, and reconnect with my intentions today?

Y / N

What spiritual lesson(s) did I learn today?

Which of Allah's names or attributes did you feel most connected to today? Why?

Did you let go of anything today that was weighing on your heart?

Something I will do for self-care tomorrow is...

To be a better version of myself tomorrow, inshaAllah I will...

additional notes

DAY 3
ramadan

"My servants who have transgressed against themselves [by sinning], do not despair of the mercy of Allah. Indeed, Allah forgives all sins. Indeed, it is He who is the Forgiving, the Merciful."

—The Quran (39:53)

Thoughts I choose to release as I begin today...

Take a moment to jot down everything on your mind—tasks, worries, grudges, anything at all. This quick exercise will help you begin your day with a clear heart & mind.

ramadan
DAY 3

my schedule

12 AM
1 AM
2 AM
3 AM
4 AM
5 AM
6 AM
7 AM
8 AM
9 AM
10 AM
11 AM
12 PM
1 PM
2 PM
3 PM
4 PM
5 PM
6 PM
7 PM
8 PM
9 PM
10 PM
11 PM

are you fasting today?

○ YES   ○ NO, I'M EXCUSED

DID YOU PAY YOUR FIDYAH? Y / N

suhoor ☼

iftar ☾

workout

○ YES   ○ NO

did you know...

Fasting supports heart health by lowering cholesterol and blood pressure.

daily Quran:

	JUZZ	CHAPTER	VERSE
START:			
FINISH:			

good deeds:

○ I GAVE IN CHARITY   ○ I VISITED A SICK PERSON
○ I HELPED SOMEONE IN NEED   ○ I DID A SECRET GOOD DEED
○ I FORGAVE SOMEONE   ○ I SPOKE WITH MY PARENTS
○ I FED A HUNGRY PERSON   ○ I HOSTED IFTAR

prayers

○ FAJR   ○ ISHA
○ DHUR   ○ TARAWEEH
○ ASR   ○ TAHAJJUD
○ MAGHRIB

adhkaar

○ MORNING
○ EVENING

additional notes

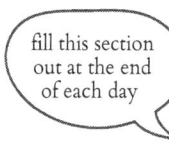

fill this section
out at the end
of each day

A moment for
Mindfulness

Now let's check-in with how you're feeling spiritually and emotionally...

I am feeling...

ANGRY   TIRED   SAD   HAPPY   EXCITED

I feel this way right now because...

Alhamdulillah for...

Have I taken a moment to pause,
breathe, and reconnect with my
intentions today?

Y / N

What spiritual lesson(s) did I learn today?

Which of Allah's names or attributes did
you feel most connected to today? Why?

Did you let go of anything today that
was weighing on your heart?

Something I will do for
self-care tomorrow is...

To be a better version of myself
tomorrow, inshaAllah I will...

additional notes

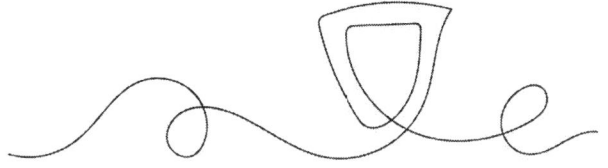

DAY 4
ramadan

"Fasting is a shield. If any one of you is fasting, let him no utter obscene talk or raise his voice in anger, and if anyone insults him or wants to fight, let him say: *I am fasting.*"

[Nasa'i 2216]

Thoughts I choose to release as I begin today...

Take a moment to jot down everything on your mind—tasks, worries, grudges, anything at all. This quick exercise will help you begin your day with a clear heart & mind.

ramadan
DAY 4

_____

my schedule

12 AM

1 AM

2 AM

3 AM

4 AM

5 AM

6 AM

7 AM

8 AM

9 AM

10 AM

11 AM

12 PM

1 PM

2 PM

3 PM

4 PM

5 PM

6 PM

7 PM

8 PM

9 PM

10 PM

11 PM

are you fasting today?

○ YES   ○ NO, I'M EXCUSED

DID YOU PAY YOUR FIDYAH? Y / N

suhoor ☀

_____
_____
_____

iftar ☾

_____
_____
_____

workout

○ YES   ○ NO

💡 _did you know..._

Fasting can enhance your body's ability to burn fat, aiding in weight management.

daily Quran:

	JUZZ	CHAPTER	VERSE
START:			
FINISH:			

good deeds:

○ I GAVE IN CHARITY   ○ I VISITED A SICK PERSON

○ I HELPED SOMEONE IN NEED   ○ I DID A SECRET GOOD DEED

○ I FORGAVE SOMEONE   ○ I SPOKE WITH MY PARENTS

○ I FED A HUNGRY PERSON   ○ I HOSTED IFTAR

prayers

○ FAJR   ○ ISHA

○ DHUR   ○ TARAWEEH

○ ASR   ○ TAHAJJUD

○ MAGHRIB

adhkaar

○ MORNING

○ EVENING

additional notes

A moment for
Mindfulness

fill this section out at the end of each day

Now let's check-in with how you're feeling spiritually and emotionally...

I am feeling...

ANGRY · TIRED · SAD · HAPPY · EXCITED

I feel this way right now because...

Alhamdulillah for...

Have I taken a moment to pause, breathe, and reconnect with my intentions today?

Y / N

What spiritual lesson(s) did I learn today?

Which of Allah's names or attributes did you feel most connected to today? Why?

Did you let go of anything today that was weighing on your heart?

Something I will do for self-care tomorrow is...

To be a better version of myself tomorrow, inshaAllah I will...

additional notes

DAY 5
ramadan

"The believers who show the most perfect Faith are those
who have the best behavior, and the best of you are those
who are the best to their wives."

[Tirmidhi]

Thoughts I choose to release as I begin today...

Take a moment to jot down everything on your mind—tasks, worries, grudges, anything at all. This quick exercise will help you begin your day with a clear heart & mind.

_____

_____

_____

_____

_____

_____

_____

_____

_____

_____

_____

_____

_____

_____

_____

_____

_____

my schedule

12 AM

1 AM

2 AM

3 AM

4 AM

5 AM

6 AM

7 AM

8 AM

9 AM

10 AM

11 AM

12 PM

1 PM

2 PM

3 PM

4 PM

5 PM

6 PM

7 PM

8 PM

9 PM

10 PM

11 PM

---

are you fasting today?

○ YES   ○ NO, I'M EXCUSED

DID YOU PAY YOUR FIDYAH? Y / N

suhoor ☀

iftar ☾

workout

○ YES   ○ NO

did you know...

Fasting can make your body respond better to insulin, helping control blood sugar levels.

daily Quran:

	JUZZ	CHAPTER	VERSE
START:			
FINISH:			

good deeds:

○ I GAVE IN CHARITY   ○ I VISITED A SICK PERSON

○ I HELPED SOMEONE IN NEED   ○ I DID A SECRET GOOD DEED

○ I FORGAVE SOMEONE   ○ I SPOKE WITH MY PARENTS

○ I FED A HUNGRY PERSON   ○ I HOSTED IFTAR

prayers

○ FAJR   ○ ISHA

○ DHUR   ○ TARAWEEH

○ ASR   ○ TAHAJJUD

○ MAGHRIB

adhkaar

○ MORNING

○ EVENING

additional notes

fill this section out at the end of each day

A moment for
Mindfulness

Now let's check-in with how you're feeling spiritually and emotionally...

I am feeling...

ANGRY   TIRED   SAD   HAPPY EXCITED

I feel this way right now because...

Alhamdulillah for...

Have I taken a moment to pause, breathe, and reconnect with my intentions today?

Y / N

What spiritual lesson(s) did I learn today?

Which of Allah's names or attributes did you feel most connected to today? Why?

Did you let go of anything today that was weighing on your heart?

Something I will do for self-care tomorrow is...

To be a better version of myself tomorrow, inshaAllah I will...

additional notes

DAY 6
ramadan

"Indeed, in the creation of the heavens and the earth and the alternation of the night and the day are signs for those of understanding. Who remember Allah while standing or sitting or [lying] on their sides and give thought to the creation of the heavens and the earth, [saying], "Our Lord, You did not create this aimlessly; exalted are You [above such a thing]; then protect us from the punishment of the Fire."

—The Quran (3:190-191)

Thoughts I choose to release as I begin today...

Take a moment to jot down everything on your mind—tasks, worries, grudges, anything at all. This quick exercise will help you begin your day with a clear heart & mind.

ramadan
DAY 6

my schedule

12 AM

1 AM

2 AM

3 AM

4 AM

5 AM

6 AM

7 AM

8 AM

9 AM

10 AM

11 AM

12 PM

1 PM

2 PM

3 PM

4 PM

5 PM

6 PM

7 PM

8 PM

9 PM

10 PM

11 PM

are you fasting today?

○ YES   ○ NO, I'M EXCUSED

DID YOU PAY YOUR FIDYAH? Y / N

suhoor ☀

iftar ☾

workout

○ YES   ○ NO

did you know...

Fasting gives your digestive system a break allows your gut lining to repair itself, improving overall digestion.

daily Quran:

	JUZZ	CHAPTER	VERSE
START:			
FINISH:			

good deeds:

○ I GAVE IN CHARITY   ○ I VISITED A SICK PERSON

○ I HELPED SOMEONE IN NEED   ○ I DID A SECRET GOOD DEED

○ I FORGAVE SOMEONE   ○ I SPOKE WITH MY PARENTS

○ I FED A HUNGRY PERSON   ○ I HOSTED IFTAR

prayers

○ FAJR   ○ ISHA

○ DHUR   ○ TARAWEEH

○ ASR   ○ TAHAJJUD

○ MAGHRIB

adhkaar

○ MORNING

○ EVENING

additional notes

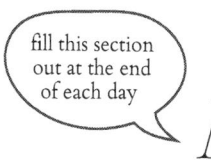

fill this section out at the end of each day

A moment for
Mindfulness

Now let's check-in with how you're feeling spiritually and emotionally...

I am feeling...

ANGRY TIRED SAD HAPPY EXCITED

I feel this way right now because...

Alhamdulillah for...

Have I taken a moment to pause, breathe, and reconnect with my intentions today?

Y / N

What spiritual lesson(s) did I learn today?

Which of Allah's names or attributes did you feel most connected to today? Why?

Did you let go of anything today that was weighing on your heart?

Something I will do for self-care tomorrow is...

To be a better version of myself tomorrow, inshaAllah I will...

additional notes

DAY 7
ramadan

"Every deed of the son of Adam will be multiplied for him, between ten and seven hundred times for each merit. Allah said: 'Except for fasting, for it is for Me and I shall reward for it.'"

[Ibn Majah 3823]

Thoughts I choose to release as I begin today...

Take a moment to jot down everything on your mind—tasks, worries, grudges, anything at all. This quick exercise will help you begin your day with a clear heart & mind.

ramadan
DAY 7

my schedule

12 AM

1 AM

2 AM

3 AM

4 AM

5 AM

6 AM

7 AM

8 AM

9 AM

10 AM

11 AM

12 PM

1 PM

2 PM

3 PM

4 PM

5 PM

6 PM

7 PM

8 PM

9 PM

10 PM

11 PM

are you fasting today?

○ YES   ○ NO, I'M EXCUSED

DID YOU PAY YOUR FIDYAH? Y / N

suhoor ☀

iftar ☾

workout

◯ YES   ○ NO

did you know...

Fasting lowers harmful molecules in the body, reducing damage to your cells.

daily Quran:

	JUZZ	CHAPTER	VERSE
START:			
FINISH:			

good deeds:

○ I GAVE IN CHARITY   ○ I VISITED A SICK PERSON

○ I HELPED SOMEONE IN NEED   ○ I DID A SECRET GOOD DEED

○ I FORGAVE SOMEONE   ○ I SPOKE WITH MY PARENTS

○ I FED A HUNGRY PERSON   ○ I HOSTED IFTAR

prayers

○ FAJR   ○ ISHA

○ DHUR   ○ TARAWEEH

○ ASR   ○ TAHAJJUD

○ MAGHRIB

adhkaar

○ MORNING

○ EVENING

additional notes

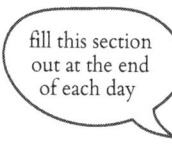

fill this section out at the end of each day

A moment for
Mindfulness

Now let's check-in with how you're feeling spiritually and emotionally...

I am feeling...

ANGRY TIRED SAD HAPPY EXCITED

I feel this way right now because...

Alhamdulillah for...

Have I taken a moment to pause, breathe, and reconnect with my intentions today?

Y / N

What spiritual lesson(s) did I learn today?

Which of Allah's names or attributes did you feel most connected to today? Why?

Did you let go of anything today that was weighing on your heart?

Something I will do for self-care tomorrow is...

To be a better version of myself tomorrow, inshaAllah I will...

additional notes

DAY 8
ramadan

"Righteousness is not that you turn your faces toward the east or the west, but [true] righteousness is [in] one who believes in Allah, the Last Day, the angels, the Book, and the prophets and gives wealth, in spite of love for it, to relatives, orphans, the needy, the traveler, those who ask [for help], and for freeing slaves; [and who] establishes prayer and gives zakah; [those who] fulfill their promise when they promise; and [those who] are patient in poverty and hardship and during battle. Those are the ones who have been true, and it is those who are the righteous."

—The Quran (2:177)

Thoughts I choose to release as I begin today...

Take a moment to jot down everything on your mind—tasks, worries, grudges, anything at all. This quick exercise will help you begin your day with a clear heart & mind.

ramadan
DAY 8

my schedule

12 AM

1 AM

2 AM

3 AM

4 AM

5 AM

6 AM

7 AM

8 AM

9 AM

10 AM

11 AM

12 PM

1 PM

2 PM

3 PM

4 PM

5 PM

6 PM

7 PM

8 PM

9 PM

10 PM

11 PM

are you fasting today?

◯ YES   ◯ NO, I'M EXCUSED

DID YOU PAY YOUR FIDYAH? Y / N

suhoor ☀

iftar ☾

workout

◯ YES   ◯ NO

💡 *did you know...*

Studies show fasting may activate genes that help with longevity and slowing the aging process.

daily Quran:

	JUZZ	CHAPTER	VERSE
START:			
FINISH:			

good deeds:

◯ I GAVE IN CHARITY   ◯ I VISITED A SICK PERSON

◯ I HELPED SOMEONE IN NEED   ◯ I DID A SECRET GOOD DEED

◯ I FORGAVE SOMEONE   ◯ I SPOKE WITH MY PARENTS

◯ I FED A HUNGRY PERSON   ◯ I HOSTED IFTAR

prayers

◯ FAJR   ◯ ISHA

◯ DHUR   ◯ TARAWEEH

◯ ASR   ◯ TAHAJJUD

◯ MAGHRIB

adhkaar

◯ MORNING

◯ EVENING

additional notes

fill this section out at the end of each day

A moment for
Mindfulness

Now let's check-in with how you're feeling spiritually and emotionally...

I am feeling...

ANGRY TIRED SAD HAPPY EXCITED

I feel this way right now because...

Alhamdulillah for...

Have I taken a moment to pause, breathe, and reconnect with my intentions today?

Y / N

What spiritual lesson(s) did I learn today?

Which of Allah's names or attributes did you feel most connected to today? Why?

Did you let go of anything today that was weighing on your heart?

Something I will do for self-care tomorrow is...

To be a better version of myself tomorrow, inshaAllah I will...

additional notes

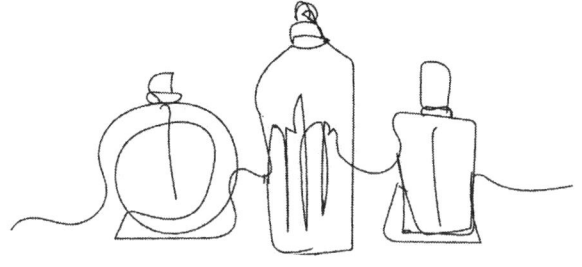

DAY 9
ramadan

"By the One in whose hand is the soul of Muhammad, the smell coming from the mouth of the fasting person is better before Allah than the fragrance of musk."

[Nasa'i 2216]

Thoughts I choose to release as I begin today...

Take a moment to jot down everything on your mind—tasks, worries, grudges, anything at all. This quick exercise will help you begin your day with a clear heart & mind.

ramadan
DAY 9

my schedule

12 AM

1 AM

2 AM

3 AM

4 AM

5 AM

6 AM

7 AM

8 AM

9 AM

10 AM

11 AM

12 PM

1 PM

2 PM

3 PM

4 PM

5 PM

6 PM

7 PM

8 PM

9 PM

10 PM

11 PM

are you fasting today?

○ YES   ○ NO, I'M EXCUSED

DID YOU PAY YOUR FIDYAH? Y / N

suhoor ☀

iftar ☾

workout

○ YES   ○ NO

💡 did you know...

Fasting can help regulate your sleep-wake cycle, promoting better rest.

daily Quran:

	JUZZ	CHAPTER	VERSE
START:			
FINISH:			

good deeds:

○ I GAVE IN CHARITY   ○ I VISITED A SICK PERSON
○ I HELPED SOMEONE IN NEED   ○ I DID A SECRET GOOD DEED
○ I FORGAVE SOMEONE   ○ I SPOKE WITH MY PARENTS
○ I FED A HUNGRY PERSON   ○ I HOSTED IFTAR

prayers

○ FAJR   ○ ISHA
○ DHUR   ○ TARAWEEH
○ ASR   ○ TAHAJJUD
○ MAGHRIB

adhkaar

○ MORNING
○ EVENING

additional notes

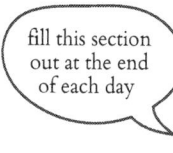

fill this section out at the end of each day

A moment for
Mindfulness

Now let's check-in with how you're feeling spiritually and emotionally...

I am feeling...

ANGRY   TIRED   SAD   HAPPY   EXCITED

I feel this way right now because...

Alhamdulillah for...

Have I taken a moment to pause, breathe, and reconnect with my intentions today?

Y / N

What spiritual lesson(s) did I learn today?

Which of Allah's names or attributes did you feel most connected to today? Why?

Did you let go of anything today that was weighing on your heart?

Something I will do for self-care tomorrow is...

To be a better version of myself tomorrow, inshaAllah I will...

additional notes

DAY 10
ramadan

"[Fasting for] a limited number of days. So whoever among you is ill or on a journey [during them]—then an equal number of days [are to be made up]. And upon those who are able [to fast, but with hardship]—a ransom [as substitute] of feeding a poor person [each day]. And whoever volunteers excess—it is better for him. But to fast is best for you, if you only knew."

—The Quran (2:184)

Thoughts I choose to release as I begin today...

Take a moment to jot down everything on your mind—tasks, worries, grudges, anything at all. This quick exercise will help you begin your day with a clear heart & mind.

ramadan
DAY 10

my schedule

12 AM

1 AM

2 AM

3 AM

4 AM

5 AM

6 AM

7 AM

8 AM

9 AM

10 AM

11 AM

12 PM

1 PM

2 PM

3 PM

4 PM

5 PM

6 PM

7 PM

8 PM

9 PM

10 PM

11 PM

---

are you fasting today?

○ YES   ○ NO, I'M EXCUSED

DID YOU PAY YOUR FIDYAH? Y / N

suhoor ☀

iftar ☾

workout

○ YES   ○ NO

💡 *did you know...*

Regular fasting is linked to a healthier heart, reducing the risk of cardiovascular diseases

daily Quran:

	JUZZ	CHAPTER	VERSE
START:			
FINISH:			

good deeds:

○ I GAVE IN CHARITY   ○ I VISITED A SICK PERSON

○ I HELPED SOMEONE IN NEED   ○ I DID A SECRET GOOD DEED

○ I FORGAVE SOMEONE   ○ I SPOKE WITH MY PARENTS

○ I FED A HUNGRY PERSON   ○ I HOSTED IFTAR

prayers

○ FAJR   ○ ISHA

○ DHUR   ○ TARAWEEH

○ ASR   ○ TAHAJJUD

○ MAGHRIB

adhkaar

○ MORNING

○ EVENING

additional notes

fill this section out at the end of each day

A moment for
Mindfulness

Now let's check-in with how you're feeling spiritually and emotionally...

I am feeling...

ANGRY   TIRED   SAD   HAPPY   EXCITED

I feel this way right now because...

Alhamdulillah for...

Have I taken a moment to pause, breathe, and reconnect with my intentions today?

Y / N

What spiritual lesson(s) did I learn today?

Which of Allah's names or attributes did you feel most connected to today? Why?

Did you let go of anything today that was weighing on your heart?

Something I will do for self-care tomorrow is...

To be a better version of myself tomorrow, inshaAllah I will...

additional notes

DAY 11
ramadan

"The example of those who spend their wealth in the way
of Allah is like a seed [of grain] that sprouts seven ears; in
every ear is a hundred grains. And Allah multiplies [His
reward] for whom He wills. And Allah is all-
Encompassing and Knowing."

—The Quran (2:261)

Thoughts I choose to release as I begin today...

Take a moment to jot down everything on your mind—tasks, worries, grudges, anything at all. This quick exercise will help you begin your day with a clear heart & mind.

ramadan
DAY 11

my schedule

12 AM

1 AM

2 AM

3 AM

4 AM

5 AM

6 AM

7 AM

8 AM

9 AM

10 AM

11 AM

12 PM

1 PM

2 PM

3 PM

4 PM

5 PM

6 PM

7 PM

8 PM

9 PM

10 PM

11 PM

are you fasting today?

○ YES   ○ NO, I'M EXCUSED

DID YOU PAY YOUR FIDYAH? Y / N

suhoor ☀

iftar ☾

workout

○   YES   ○   NO

did you know...

The need to rehydrate properly during non-fasting hours encourages better water consumption habits.

daily Quran:

	JUZZ	CHAPTER	VERSE
START:			
FINISH:			

good deeds:

○ I GAVE IN CHARITY   ○ I VISITED A SICK PERSON

○ I HELPED SOMEONE IN NEED   ○ I DID A SECRET GOOD DEED

○ I FORGAVE SOMEONE   ○ I SPOKE WITH MY PARENTS

○ I FED A HUNGRY PERSON   ○ I HOSTED IFTAR

prayers

○ FAJR   ○ ISHA

○ DHUR   ○ TARAWEEH

○ ASR   ○ TAHAJJUD

○ MAGHRIB

adhkaar

○   MORNING

○   EVENING

additional notes

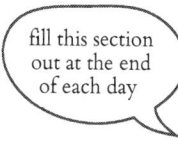

fill this section
out at the end
of each day

A moment for
Mindfulness

Now let's check-in with how you're feeling spiritually and emotionally...

I am feeling...

ANGRY   TIRED   SAD   HAPPY EXCITED

I feel this way right now because...

Alhamdulillah for...

Have I taken a moment to pause,
breathe, and reconnect with my
intentions today?

Y / N

What spiritual lesson(s) did I learn today?

Which of Allah's names or attributes did
you feel most connected to today? Why?

Did you let go of anything today that
was weighing on your heart?

Something I will do for
self-care tomorrow is...

To be a better version of myself
tomorrow, inshaAllah I will...

additional notes

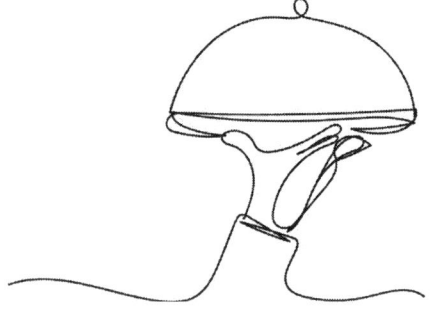

DAY 12
ramadan

"Whoever provides the food for a fasting person to break his fast with, then for him is the same reward as his (the fasting person's), without anything being diminished from the reward of the fasting person."

[Tirmidhi 807]

Thoughts I choose to release as I begin today...

Take a moment to jot down everything on your mind—tasks, worries, grudges, anything at all. This quick exercise will help you begin your day with a clear heart & mind.

ramadan
DAY 12

my schedule

12 AM

1 AM

2 AM

3 AM

4 AM

5 AM

6 AM

7 AM

8 AM

9 AM

10 AM

11 AM

12 PM

1 PM

2 PM

3 PM

4 PM

5 PM

6 PM

7 PM

8 PM

9 PM

10 PM

11 PM

are you fasting today?

○ YES   ○ NO, I'M EXCUSED

DID YOU PAY YOUR FIDYAH? Y / N

suhoor ☀

iftar ☾

workout

○ YES   ○ NO

did you know...

Fasting stimulates the production of human growth hormone, which supports metabolism and muscle strength.

daily Quran:

	JUZZ	CHAPTER	VERSE
START:			
FINISH:			

good deeds:

○ I GAVE IN CHARITY   ○ I VISITED A SICK PERSON

○ I HELPED SOMEONE IN NEED   ○ I DID A SECRET GOOD DEED

○ I FORGAVE SOMEONE   ○ I SPOKE WITH MY PARENTS

○ I FED A HUNGRY PERSON   ○ I HOSTED IFTAR

prayers

○ FAJR   ○ ISHA

○ DHUR   ○ TARAWEEH

○ ASR   ○ TAHAJJUD

○ MAGHRIB

adhkaar

○ MORNING

○ EVENING

additional notes

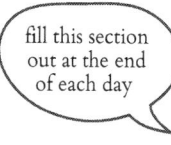

fill this section out at the end of each day

A moment for
Mindfulness

Now let's check-in with how you're feeling spiritually and emotionally...

I am feeling...

ANGRY   TIRED   SAD   HAPPY   EXCITED

I feel this way right now because...

Alhamdulillah for...

Have I taken a moment to pause, breathe, and reconnect with my intentions today?

Y / N

What spiritual lesson(s) did I learn today?

Which of Allah's names or attributes did you feel most connected to today? Why?

Did you let go of anything today that was weighing on your heart?

Something I will do for self-care tomorrow is...

To be a better version of myself tomorrow, inshaAllah I will...

additional notes

DAY 13
ramadan

"Know that this worldly life is no more than play,
amusement, luxury, mutual boasting, and competition in
wealth and children. This is like rain that causes plants to
grow, to the delight of the planters. But later the plants dry
up and you see them wither, then they are reduced to chaff.
And in the Hereafter there will be either severe punishment
or forgiveness and pleasure of Allah, whereas the life of this
world is no more than the delusion of enjoyment."

—The Quran (57:20)

Thoughts I choose to release as I begin today...

Take a moment to jot down everything on your mind—tasks, worries, grudges, anything at all. This quick exercise will help you begin your day with a clear heart & mind.

ramadan
DAY 13

my schedule

12 AM

1 AM

2 AM

3 AM

4 AM

5 AM

6 AM

7 AM

8 AM

9 AM

10 AM

11 AM

12 PM

1 PM

2 PM

3 PM

4 PM

5 PM

6 PM

7 PM

8 PM

9 PM

10 PM

11 PM

are you fasting today?

○ YES   ○ NO, I'M EXCUSED

DID YOU PAY YOUR FIDYAH? Y / N

suhoor ☼

iftar ☾

workout

○ YES   ○ NO

did you know...

Fasting can reset your taste buds and reduce dependence on sugary or processed foods.

daily Quran:

	JUZZ	CHAPTER	VERSE
START:			
FINISH:			

good deeds:

○ I GAVE IN CHARITY   ○ I VISITED A SICK PERSON

○ I HELPED SOMEONE IN NEED   ○ I DID A SECRET GOOD DEED

○ I FORGAVE SOMEONE   ○ I SPOKE WITH MY PARENTS

○ I FED A HUNGRY PERSON   ○ I HOSTED IFTAR

prayers

○ FAJR   ○ ISHA

○ DHUR   ○ TARAWEEH

○ ASR   ○ TAHAJJUD

○ MAGHRIB

adhkaar

○ MORNING

○ EVENING

additional notes

fill this section
out at the end
of each day

A moment for
Mindfulness

Now let's check-in with how you're feeling spiritually and emotionally...

I am feeling...

ANGRY   TIRED   SAD   HAPPY   EXCITED

I feel this way right now because...

Alhamdulillah for...

Have I taken a moment to pause, breathe, and reconnect with my intentions today?

Y / N

What spiritual lesson(s) did I learn today?

Which of Allah's names or attributes did you feel most connected to today? Why?

Did you let go of anything today that was weighing on your heart?

Something I will do for self-care tomorrow is...

To be a better version of myself tomorrow, inshaAllah I will...

additional notes

DAY 14
ramadan

"Whoever prays during the night in Ramadan out
of sincere faith and seeking its reward from Allah,
will have all of his previous sins forgiven."

[Bukhari]

Thoughts I choose to release as I begin today...

Take a moment to jot down everything on your mind—tasks, worries, grudges, anything at all. This quick exercise will help you begin your day with a clear heart & mind.

ramadan
DAY 14

my schedule

12 AM

1 AM

2 AM

3 AM

4 AM

5 AM

6 AM

7 AM

8 AM

9 AM

10 AM

11 AM

12 PM

1 PM

2 PM

3 PM

4 PM

5 PM

6 PM

7 PM

8 PM

9 PM

10 PM

11 PM

are you fasting today?

○ YES   ○ NO, I'M EXCUSED

DID YOU PAY YOUR FIDYAH? Y / N

suhoor ☼

iftar ☾

workout

○ YES   ○ NO

did you know...

Early research indicates fasting may inhibit cancer cell growth by depriving them of nutrients.

daily Quran:

	JUZZ	CHAPTER	VERSE
START:			
FINISH:			

good deeds:

○ I GAVE IN CHARITY   ○ I VISITED A SICK PERSON
○ I HELPED SOMEONE IN NEED   ○ I DID A SECRET GOOD DEED
○ I FORGAVE SOMEONE   ○ I SPOKE WITH MY PARENTS
○ I FED A HUNGRY PERSON   ○ I HOSTED IFTAR

prayers

○ FAJR   ○ ISHA
○ DHUR   ○ TARAWEEH
○ ASR   ○ TAHAJJUD
○ MAGHRIB

adhkaar

○ MORNING
○ EVENING

additional notes

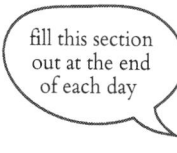
fill this section
out at the end
of each day

A moment for
Mindfulness

Now let's check-in with how you're feeling spiritually and emotionally...

I am feeling...

ANGRY TIRED SAD HAPPY EXCITED

I feel this way right now because...

Alhamdulillah for...

Have I taken a moment to pause,
breathe, and reconnect with my
intentions today?

Y / N

What spiritual lesson(s) did I learn today?

Which of Allah's names or attributes did
you feel most connected to today? Why?

Did you let go of anything today that
was weighing on your heart?

Something I will do for
self-care tomorrow is...

To be a better version of myself
tomorrow, inshaAllah I will...

additional notes

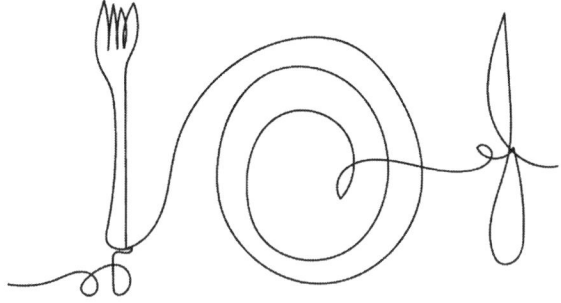

DAY 15
ramadan

"The fasting person has two moments of joy:
When he breaks his fast he rejoices at breaking his
fast and when he meets his Lord, the Mighty and
Sublime, he will rejoice at having fasted."

[Nasa'i 2216]

Thoughts I choose to release as I begin today...

Take a moment to jot down everything on your mind—tasks, worries, grudges, anything at all. This quick exercise will help you begin your day with a clear heart & mind.

ramadan
DAY 15

my schedule

12 AM

1 AM

2 AM

3 AM

4 AM

5 AM

6 AM

7 AM

8 AM

9 AM

10 AM

11 AM

12 PM

1 PM

2 PM

3 PM

4 PM

5 PM

6 PM

7 PM

8 PM

9 PM

10 PM

11 PM

---

are you fasting today?

○ YES   ○ NO, I'M EXCUSED

DID YOU PAY YOUR FIDYAH? Y / N

suhoor ☀

iftar ☾

workout

○ YES   ○ NO

💡 *did you know...*

By reducing inflammation and improving hydration awareness, fasting can contribute to clearer skin.

daily Quran:

	JUZZ	CHAPTER	VERSE
START:			
FINISH:			

good deeds:

○ I GAVE IN CHARITY   ○ I VISITED A SICK PERSON

○ I HELPED SOMEONE IN NEED   ○ I DID A SECRET GOOD DEED

○ I FORGAVE SOMEONE   ○ I SPOKE WITH MY PARENTS

○ I FED A HUNGRY PERSON   ○ I HOSTED IFTAR

prayers

○ FAJR   ○ ISHA

○ DHUR   ○ TARAWEEH

○ ASR   ○ TAHAJJUD

○ MAGHRIB

adhkaar

○ MORNING

○ EVENING

additional notes

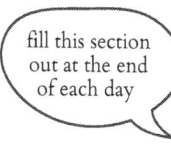

fill this section out at the end of each day

A moment for
Mindfulness

Now let's check-in with how you're feeling spiritually and emotionally...

I am feeling...

ANGRY TIRED SAD HAPPY EXCITED

I feel this way right now because...

Alhamdulillah for...

Have I taken a moment to pause, breathe, and reconnect with my intentions today?

Y / N

What spiritual lesson(s) did I learn today?

Which of Allah's names or attributes did you feel most connected to today? Why?

Did you let go of anything today that was weighing on your heart?

Something I will do for self-care tomorrow is...

To be a better version of myself tomorrow, inshaAllah I will...

additional notes

DAY 16
ramadan

"And your Lord has decreed that you not worship
except Him, and to parents, good treatment. Whether
one or both of them reach old age [while] with you, say
not to them [so much as], 'uff,' and do not repel them
but speak to them a noble word."

—The Quran (17:23)

Thoughts I choose to release as I begin today...

Take a moment to jot down everything on your mind—tasks, worries, grudges, anything at all. This quick exercise will help you begin your day with a clear heart & mind.

today's date:

my schedule

12 AM

1 AM

2 AM

3 AM

4 AM

5 AM

6 AM

7 AM

8 AM

9 AM

10 AM

11 AM

12 PM

1 PM

2 PM

3 PM

4 PM

5 PM

6 PM

7 PM

8 PM

9 PM

10 PM

11 PM

are you fasting today?

◯ YES   ◯ NO, I'M EXCUSED

DID YOU PAY YOUR FIDYAH? Y / N

suhoor ☼

iftar ☾

workout

◯ YES   ◯ NO

💡 *did you know...*

While it may seem counterintuitive, fasting often leads to more sustained energy once the body adapts.

daily Quran:

	JUZZ	CHAPTER	VERSE
START:			
FINISH:			

good deeds:

◯ I GAVE IN CHARITY   ◯ I VISITED A SICK PERSON

◯ I HELPED SOMEONE IN NEED   ◯ I DID A SECRET GOOD DEED

◯ I FORGAVE SOMEONE   ◯ I SPOKE WITH MY PARENTS

◯ I FED A HUNGRY PERSON   ◯ I HOSTED IFTAR

prayers

◯ FAJR   ◯ ISHA

◯ DHUR   ◯ TARAWEEH

◯ ASR   ◯ TAHAJJUD

◯ MAGHRIB

adhkaar

◯ MORNING

◯ EVENING

additional notes

A moment for
Mindfulness

fill this section out at the end of each day

Now let's check-in with how you're feeling spiritually and emotionally...

I am feeling...

😠 😟 😢 🙂 😄
ANGRY TIRED SAD HAPPY EXCITED

I feel this way right now because...

Alhamdulillah for...

Have I taken a moment to pause, breathe, and reconnect with my intentions today?

Y / N

What spiritual lesson(s) did I learn today?

Which of Allah's names or attributes did you feel most connected to today? Why?

Did you let go of anything today that was weighing on your heart?

Something I will do for self-care tomorrow is...

To be a better version of myself tomorrow, inshaAllah I will...

additional notes

DAY 17
ramadan

"And We will surely test you with something of fear and
hunger and a loss of wealth and lives and fruits, but give
good tidings to the patient, who, when disaster strikes
them, say, 'Indeed we belong to Allah, and indeed to
Him we will return.'"

—The Quran (2:155-156)

Thoughts I choose to release as I begin today...

Take a moment to jot down everything on your mind—tasks, worries, grudges, anything at all. This quick exercise will help you begin your day with a clear heart & mind.

ramadan
DAY 17

---

my schedule

12 AM

1 AM

2 AM

3 AM

4 AM

5 AM

6 AM

7 AM

8 AM

9 AM

10 AM

I I AM

12 PM

1 PM

2 PM

3 PM

4 PM

5 PM

6 PM

7 PM

8 PM

9 PM

10 PM

11 PM

---

are you fasting today?

○ YES   ○ NO, I'M EXCUSED

DID YOU PAY YOUR FIDYAH? Y / N

suhoor ☼

iftar ☾

workout

○ YES   ○ NO

did you know...

Fasting gives the stomach and intestines time to reset, potentially easing digestive issues.

daily Quran:

	JUZZ	CHAPTER	VERSE
START:			
FINISH:			

good deeds:

○ I GAVE IN CHARITY   ○ I VISITED A SICK PERSON

○ I HELPED SOMEONE IN NEED   ○ I DID A SECRET GOOD DEED

○ I FORGAVE SOMEONE   ○ I SPOKE WITH MY PARENTS

○ I FED A HUNGRY PERSON   ○ I HOSTED IFTAR

prayers

○ FAJR   ○ ISHA

○ DHUR   ○ TARAWEEH

○ ASR   ○ TAHAJJUD

○ MAGHRIB

adhkaar

○ MORNING

○ EVENING

additional notes

fill this section out at the end of each day

A moment for
Mindfulness

Now let's check-in with how you're feeling spiritually and emotionally...

I am feeling...

ANGRY   TIRED   SAD   HAPPY   EXCITED

I feel this way right now because...

Alhamdulillah for...

Have I taken a moment to pause, breathe, and reconnect with my intentions today?

Y / N

What spiritual lesson(s) did I learn today?

Which of Allah's names or attributes did you feel most connected to today? Why?

Did you let go of anything today that was weighing on your heart?

Something I will do for self-care tomorrow is...

To be a better version of myself tomorrow, inshaAllah I will...

additional notes

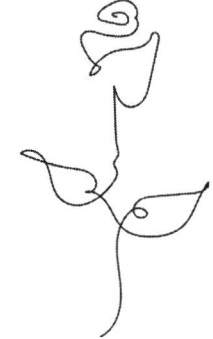

DAY 18
ramadan

"No calamity befalls a Muslim but that Allah
expiates some of his sins because of it, even though
it were the prick he receives from a thorn."

[Bukhari 5640]

Thoughts I choose to release as I begin today...

Take a moment to jot down everything on your mind—tasks, worries, grudges, anything at all. This quick exercise will help you begin your day with a clear heart & mind.

ramadan
DAY 18

my schedule

12 AM

1 AM

2 AM

3 AM

4 AM

5 AM

6 AM

7 AM

8 AM

9 AM

10 AM

11 AM

12 PM

1 PM

2 PM

3 PM

4 PM

5 PM

6 PM

7 PM

8 PM

9 PM

10 PM

11 PM

are you fasting today?

○ YES   ○ NO, I'M EXCUSED

DID YOU PAY YOUR FIDYAH? Y / N

suhoor ☀

iftar ☾

workout

○ YES   ○ NO

💡 *did you know...*

Fasting stimulates the production of human growth hormone, which supports metabolism and muscle strength.

daily Quran:

	JUZZ	CHAPTER	VERSE
START:			
FINISH:			

good deeds:

○ I GAVE IN CHARITY   ○ I VISITED A SICK PERSON

○ I HELPED SOMEONE IN NEED ○ I DID A SECRET GOOD DEED

○ I FORGAVE SOMEONE   ○ I SPOKE WITH MY PARENTS

○ I FED A HUNGRY PERSON   ○ I HOSTED IFTAR

prayers

○ FAJR   ○ ISHA

○ DHUR   ○ TARAWEEH

○ ASR   ○ TAHAJJUD

○ MAGHRIB

adhkaar

○ MORNING

○ EVENING

additional notes

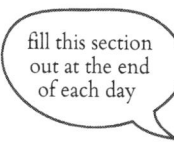

A moment for
Mindfulness

Now let's check-in with how you're feeling spiritually and emotionally...

I am feeling...

ANGRY   TIRED   SAD   HAPPY   EXCITED

I feel this way right now because...

Alhamdulillah for...

Have I taken a moment to pause, breathe, and reconnect with my intentions today?

Y / N

What spiritual lesson(s) did I learn today?

Which of Allah's names or attributes did you feel most connected to today? Why?

Did you let go of anything today that was weighing on your heart?

Something I will do for self-care tomorrow is...

To be a better version of myself tomorrow, inshaAllah I will...

additional notes

DAY 19
ramadan

"Every region has its distinct characteristic, and the
distinct characteristic of Islam is modesty."

[Ibn Majah 4181]

Thoughts I choose to release as I begin today...

Take a moment to jot down everything on your mind—tasks, worries, grudges, anything at all. This quick exercise will help you begin your day with a clear heart & mind.

ramādan
DAY 19

my schedule

12 AM

1 AM

2 AM

3 AM

4 AM

5 AM

6 AM

7 AM

8 AM

9 AM

10 AM

11 AM

12 PM

1 PM

2 PM

3 PM

4 PM

5 PM

6 PM

7 PM

8 PM

9 PM

10 PM

11 PM

are you fasting today?

○ YES   ○ NO, I'M EXCUSED

DID YOU PAY YOUR FIDYAH? Y / N

suhoor ☼

iftar ☾

workout

○ YES   ○ NO

did you know...

Fasting can regulate hunger hormones like ghrelin and leptin, helping control appetite.

daily Quran:

	JUZZ	CHAPTER	VERSE
START:			
FINISH:			

good deeds:

○ I GAVE IN CHARITY   ○ I VISITED A SICK PERSON

○ I HELPED SOMEONE IN NEED   ○ I DID A SECRET GOOD DEED

○ I FORGAVE SOMEONE   ○ I SPOKE WITH MY PARENTS

○ I FED A HUNGRY PERSON   ○ I HOSTED IFTAR

prayers

○ FAJR   ○ ISHA

○ DHUR   ○ TARAWEEH

○ ASR   ○ TAHAJJUD

○ MAGHRIB

adhkaar

○ MORNING

○ EVENING

additional notes

A moment for
Mindfulness

Now let's check-in with how you're feeling spiritually and emotionally...

I am feeling...

ANGRY   TIRED   SAD   HAPPY   EXCITED

I feel this way right now because...

Alhamdulillah for...

Have I taken a moment to pause, breathe, and reconnect with my intentions today?

Y / N

What spiritual lesson(s) did I learn today?

Which of Allah's names or attributes did you feel most connected to today? Why?

Did you let go of anything today that was weighing on your heart?

Something I will do for self-care tomorrow is...

To be a better version of myself tomorrow, inshaAllah I will...

additional notes

DAY 20
ramadan

"Search for the Night of Qadr in the odd
nights of the last ten days of Ramadan."

[Bukhari 2017]

Thoughts I choose to release as I begin today...

Take a moment to jot down everything on your mind—tasks, worries, grudges, anything at all. This quick exercise will help you begin your day with a clear heart & mind.

ramadan
DAY 20

---

my schedule

12 AM

1 AM

2 AM

3 AM

4 AM

5 AM

6 AM

7 AM

8 AM

9 AM

10 AM

11 AM

12 PM

1 PM

2 PM

3 PM

4 PM

5 PM

6 PM

7 PM

8 PM

9 PM

10 PM

11 PM

are you fasting today?

○ YES   ○ NO, I'M EXCUSED

DID YOU PAY YOUR FIDYAH? Y / N

suhoor ☀

iftar ☾

workout

○ YES   ○ NO

💡 *did you know...*

Fasting allows the liver to process and eliminate toxins more efficiently.

daily Quran:

	JUZZ	CHAPTER	VERSE
START:			
FINISH:			

good deeds:

○ I GAVE IN CHARITY   ○ I VISITED A SICK PERSON
○ I HELPED SOMEONE IN NEED   ○ I DID A SECRET GOOD DEED
○ I FORGAVE SOMEONE   ○ I SPOKE WITH MY PARENTS
○ I FED A HUNGRY PERSON   ○ I HOSTED IFTAR

prayers

○ FAJR   ○ ISHA
○ DHUR   ○ TARAWEEH
○ ASR   ○ TAHAJJUD
○ MAGHRIB

adhkaar

○ MORNING
○ EVENING

additional notes

fill this section
out at the end
of each day

A moment for
Mindfulness

Now let's check-in with how you're feeling spiritually and emotionally...

I am feeling...

ANGRY · TIRED · SAD · HAPPY · EXCITED

I feel this way right now because...

Alhamdulillah for...

Have I taken a moment to pause,
breathe, and reconnect with my
intentions today?

Y / N

What spiritual lesson(s) did I learn today?

Which of Allah's names or attributes did
you feel most connected to today? Why?

Did you let go of anything today that
was weighing on your heart?

Something I will do for
self-care tomorrow is...

To be a better version of myself
tomorrow, inshaAllah I will...

additional notes

DAY 21
ramadan

"The Night of Decree (Laylat al-Qadr) is
better than a thousand months."

—The Quran (97:3)

Thoughts I choose to release as I begin today...

Take a moment to jot down everything on your mind—tasks, worries, grudges, anything at all. This quick exercise will help you begin your day with a clear heart & mind.

_____

_____

_____

_____

_____

_____

_____

_____

_____

_____

_____

_____

_____

_____

_____

_____

_____

_____

_____

ramadan
DAY 21

my schedule

12 AM	
1 AM	
2 AM	
3 AM	
4 AM	
5 AM	
6 AM	
7 AM	
8 AM	
9 AM	
10 AM	
11 AM	
12 PM	
1 PM	
2 PM	
3 PM	
4 PM	
5 PM	
6 PM	
7 PM	
8 PM	
9 PM	
10 PM	
11 PM	

are you fasting today?

○ YES   ○ NO, I'M EXCUSED

DID YOU PAY YOUR FIDYAH? Y / N

suhoor ☀

iftar ☾

workout

○ YES   ○ NO

did you know...

Many people report heightened focus and mental clarity during tasting.

daily Quran:

	JUZZ	CHAPTER	VERSE
START:			
FINISH:			

good deeds:

○ I GAVE IN CHARITY   ○ I VISITED A SICK PERSON
○ I HELPED SOMEONE IN NEED   ○ I DID A SECRET GOOD DEED
○ I FORGAVE SOMEONE   ○ I SPOKE WITH MY PARENTS
○ I FED A HUNGRY PERSON   ○ I HOSTED IFTAR

prayers

○ FAJR   ○ ISHA
○ DHUR   ○ TARAWEEH
○ ASR   ○ TAHAJJUD
○ MAGHRIB

adhkaar

○ MORNING
○ EVENING

additional notes

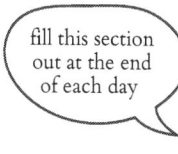

fill this section out at the end of each day

A moment for
Mindfulness

Now let's check-in with how you're feeling spiritually and emotionally...

I am feeling...

😠 😫 😔 🙂 😆
ANGRY · TIRED · SAD · HAPPY · EXCITED

I feel this way right now because...

Alhamdulillah for...

Have I taken a moment to pause, breathe, and reconnect with my intentions today?

Y / N

What spiritual lesson(s) did I learn today?

Which of Allah's names or attributes did you feel most connected to today? Why?

Did you let go of anything today that was weighing on your heart?

Something I will do for self-care tomorrow is...

To be a better version of myself tomorrow, inshaAllah I will...

additional notes

DAY 22
ramadan

"Whoever does not give up false statements
(i.e. telling lies), and evil deeds, and speaking
bad words to others, Allah is not in need of
his (fasting) leaving his food and drink."

[Bukhari 6057]

Thoughts I choose to release as I begin today...

Take a moment to jot down everything on your mind—tasks, worries, grudges, anything at all. This quick exercise will help you begin your day with a clear heart & mind.

ramadan
DAY 22

my schedule

12 AM

1 AM

2 AM

3 AM

4 AM

5 AM

6 AM

7 AM

8 AM

9 AM

10 AM

11 AM

12 PM

1 PM

2 PM

3 PM

4 PM

5 PM

6 PM

7 PM

8 PM

9 PM

10 PM

11 PM

are you fasting today?

○ YES   ○ NO, I'M EXCUSED

DID YOU PAY YOUR FIDYAH? Y / N

suhoor ☼

iftar ☾

workout

○ YES   ○ NO

did you know...

When fasting, your body starts to burn fat for energy, entering a state called ketosis, which can help with fat loss.

daily Quran:

	JUZZ	CHAPTER	VERSE
START:			
FINISH:			

good deeds:

○ I GAVE IN CHARITY   ○ I VISITED A SICK PERSON
○ I HELPED SOMEONE IN NEED   ○ I DID A SECRET GOOD DEED
○ I FORGAVE SOMEONE   ○ I SPOKE WITH MY PARENTS
○ I FED A HUNGRY PERSON   ○ I HOSTED IFTAR

prayers

○ FAJR   ○ ISHA
○ DHUR   ○ TARAWEEH
○ ASR   ○ TAHAJJUD
○ MAGHRIB

adhkaar

○ MORNING

○ EVENING

additional notes

fill this section out at the end of each day

A moment for
Mindfulness

Now let's check-in with how you're feeling spiritually and emotionally...

I am feeling...

ANGRY   TIRED   SAD   HAPPY   EXCITED

I feel this way right now because...

Alhamdulillah for...

Have I taken a moment to pause, breathe, and reconnect with my intentions today?

Y / N

What spiritual lesson(s) did I learn today?

Which of Allah's names or attributes did you feel most connected to today? Why?

Did you let go of anything today that was weighing on your heart?

Something I will do for self-care tomorrow is...

To be a better version of myself tomorrow, inshaAllah I will...

additional notes

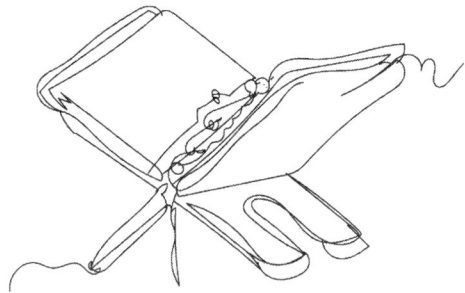

DAY 23
ramadan

"Whoever recites Ayat al-Kursi at the end of
every obligatory prayer, nothing but death
will prevent him from entering Paradise."

[Nasai]

Thoughts I choose to release as I begin today...

Take a moment to jot down everything on your mind—tasks, worries, grudges, anything at all. This quick exercise will help you begin your day with a clear heart & mind.

ramadan
DAY 23

my schedule

12 AM

1 AM

2 AM

3 AM

4 AM

5 AM

6 AM

7 AM

8 AM

9 AM

10 AM

11 AM

12 PM

1 PM

2 PM

3 PM

4 PM

5 PM

6 PM

7 PM

8 PM

9 PM

10 PM

11 PM

are you fasting today?

○ YES   ○ NO, I'M EXCUSED

DID YOU PAY YOUR FIDYAH? Y / N

suhoor ☼

iftar ☾

workout

○ YES   ○ NO

did you know...

When fasting, your body starts to burn fat for energy, entering a state called ketosis, which can help with fat loss.

daily Quran:

	JUZZ	CHAPTER	VERSE
START:			
FINISH:			

good deeds:

○ I GAVE IN CHARITY   ○ I VISITED A SICK PERSON

○ I HELPED SOMEONE IN NEED   ○ I DID A SECRET GOOD DEED

○ I FORGAVE SOMEONE   ○ I SPOKE WITH MY PARENTS

○ I FED A HUNGRY PERSON   ○ I HOSTED IFTAR

prayers

○ FAJR   ○ ISHA

○ DHUR   ○ TARAWEEH

○ ASR   ○ TAHAJJUD

○ MAGHRIB

adhkaar

○ MORNING

○ EVENING

additional notes

fill this section
out at the end
of each day

A moment for
Mindfulness

Now let's check-in with how you're feeling spiritually and emotionally...

I am feeling...

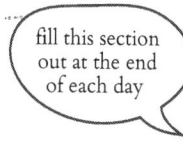

ANGRY   TIRED   SAD   HAPPY EXCITED

I feel this way right now because...

Alhamdulillah for...

Have I taken a moment to pause, breathe, and reconnect with my intentions today?

Y / N

What spiritual lesson(s) did I learn today?

Which of Allah's names or attributes did you feel most connected to today? Why?

Did you let go of anything today that was weighing on your heart?

Something I will do for self-care tomorrow is...

To be a better version of myself tomorrow, inshaAllah I will...

additional notes

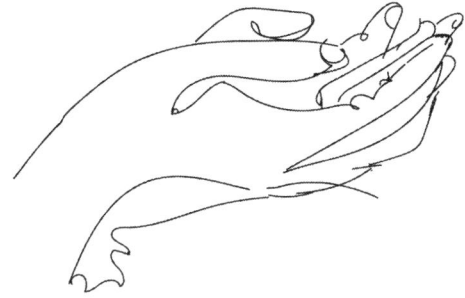

DAY 24
ramadan

"There are three whose supplication is not rejected: The fasting person when he breaks his fast, the just leader, and the supplication of the oppressed person; Allah raises it up above the clouds and opens the gates of heaven to it. And the Lord says: 'By My might, I shall surely aid you, even if it should be after a while.'"

[Tirmidhi 3598]

Thoughts I choose to release as I begin today...

Take a moment to jot down everything on your mind—tasks, worries, grudges, anything at all. This quick exercise will help you begin your day with a clear heart & mind.

ramadan
DAY 24

my schedule

12 AM	
1 AM	
2 AM	
3 AM	
4 AM	
5 AM	
6 AM	
7 AM	
8 AM	
9 AM	
10 AM	
11 AM	
12 PM	
1 PM	
2 PM	
3 PM	
4 PM	
5 PM	
6 PM	
7 PM	
8 PM	
9 PM	
10 PM	
11 PM	

are you fasting today?

○ YES   ○ NO, I'M EXCUSED

DID YOU PAY YOUR FIDYAH? Y / N

suhoor ☼

iftar ☾

workout

○ YES   ○ NO

did you know...
Fasting can promote the production of brain-derived neurotrophic factor (BDNF), which supports cognitive function and brain health.

daily Quran:

	JUZZ	CHAPTER	VERSE
START:			
FINISH:			

good deeds:

○ I GAVE IN CHARITY   ○ I VISITED A SICK PERSON
○ I HELPED SOMEONE IN NEED   ○ I DID A SECRET GOOD DEED
○ I FORGAVE SOMEONE   ○ I SPOKE WITH MY PARENTS
○ I FED A HUNGRY PERSON   ○ I HOSTED IFTAR

prayers

○ FAJR   ○ ISHA
○ DHUR   ○ TARAWEEH
○ ASR   ○ TAHAJJUD
○ MAGHRIB

adhkaar

○ MORNING
○ EVENING

additional notes

A moment for
Mindfulness

Now let's check-in with how you're feeling spiritually and emotionally...

I am feeling...

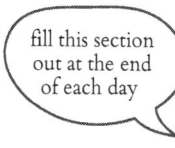

ANGRY   TIRED   SAD   HAPPY   EXCITED

I feel this way right now because...

Alhamdulillah for...

Have I taken a moment to pause, breathe, and reconnect with my intentions today?

Y / N

What spiritual lesson(s) did I learn today?

Which of Allah's names or attributes did you feel most connected to today? Why?

Did you let go of anything today that was weighing on your heart?

Something I will do for self-care tomorrow is...

To be a better version of myself tomorrow, inshaAllah I will...

additional notes

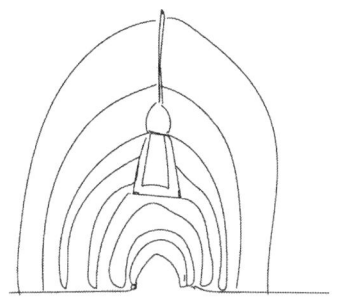

DAY 25
ramadan

"By the One in Whose Hand is my soul! You will not enter Paradise until you believe, and you will not believe until you love one another. Shall I inform you about a matter which if you do it, then you will love one another? Spread the Salam among each other."

[Tirmidhi 2688]

Thoughts I choose to release as I begin today...

Take a moment to jot down everything on your mind—tasks, worries, grudges, anything at all. This quick exercise will help you begin your day with a clear heart & mind.

_____

_____

_____

_____

_____

_____

_____

_____

_____

_____

_____

_____

_____

_____

_____

_____

_____

_____

ramadan
DAY 25

my schedule

12 AM

1 AM

2 AM

3 AM

4 AM

5 AM

6 AM

7 AM

8 AM

9 AM

10 AM

11 AM

12 PM

1 PM

2 PM

3 PM

4 PM

5 PM

6 PM

7 PM

8 PM

9 PM

10 PM

11 PM

are you fasting today?

○ YES   ○ NO, I'M EXCUSED

DID YOU PAY YOUR FIDYAH? Y / N

suhoor ☼

iftar ☾

workout

○ YES   ○ NO

did you know...

Fasting may promote the release of endorphins, the body's natural mood enhancers, leading to improved feelings of well-being and happiness.

daily Quran:

	JUZZ	CHAPTER	VERSE
START:			
FINISH:			

good deeds:

○ I GAVE IN CHARITY   ○ I VISITED A SICK PERSON

○ I HELPED SOMEONE IN NEED   ○ I DID A SECRET GOOD DEED

○ I FORGAVE SOMEONE   ○ I SPOKE WITH MY PARENTS

○ I FED A HUNGRY PERSON   ○ I HOSTED IFTAR

prayers

○ FAJR   ○ ISHA

○ DHUR   ○ TARAWEEH

○ ASR   ○ TAHAJJUD

○ MAGHRIB

adhkaar

○ MORNING

○ EVENING

additional notes

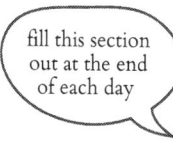

A moment for
Mindfulness

Now let's check-in with how you're feeling spiritually and emotionally...

I am feeling...

ANGRY   TIRED   SAD   HAPPY   EXCITED

I feel this way right now because...

Alhamdulillah for...

Have I taken a moment to pause, breathe, and reconnect with my intentions today?

Y / N

What spiritual lesson(s) did I learn today?

Which of Allah's names or attributes did you feel most connected to today? Why?

Did you let go of anything today that was weighing on your heart?

Something I will do for self-care tomorrow is...

To be a better version of myself tomorrow, inshaAllah I will...

additional notes

DAY 26
ramadan

"You must be gentle. Verily, gentleness is not
in anything except that it beautifies it, and it is
not removed from anything except that it
disgraces it."

[Abi Dawud 4808]

Thoughts I choose to release as I begin today...

Take a moment to jot down everything on your mind—tasks, worries, grudges, anything at all. This quick exercise will help you begin your day with a clear heart & mind.

ramadan
DAY 26

my schedule

12 AM

1 AM

2 AM

3 AM

4 AM

5 AM

6 AM

7 AM

8 AM

9 AM

10 AM

11 AM

12 PM

1 PM

2 PM

3 PM

4 PM

5 PM

6 PM

7 PM

8 PM

9 PM

10 PM

11 PM

are you fasting today?

◯ YES   ◯ NO, I'M EXCUSED

DID YOU PAY YOUR FIDYAH? Y / N

suhoor ☀

iftar ☾

workout

◯ YES   ◯ NO

did you know...

The ability to delay gratification and manage hunger can help improve emotional regulation and resilience to stressors.

daily Quran:

	JUZZ	CHAPTER	VERSE
START:			
FINISH:			

good deeds:

◯ I GAVE IN CHARITY   ◯ I VISITED A SICK PERSON

◯ I HELPED SOMEONE IN NEED   ◯ I DID A SECRET GOOD DEED

◯ I FORGAVE SOMEONE   ◯ I SPOKE WITH MY PARENTS

◯ I FED A HUNGRY PERSON   ◯ I HOSTED IFTAR

prayers

◯ FAJR   ◯ ISHA

◯ DHUR   ◯ TARAWEEH

◯ ASR   ◯ TAHAJJUD

◯ MAGHRIB

adhkaar

◯ MORNING

◯ EVENING

additional notes

A moment for
Mindfulness

Now let's check-in with how you're feeling spiritually and emotionally...

I am feeling...

ANGRY   TIRED   SAD   HAPPY   EXCITED

I feel this way right now because...

Alhamdulillah for...

Have I taken a moment to pause, breathe, and reconnect with my intentions today?

Y / N

What spiritual lesson(s) did I learn today?

Which of Allah's names or attributes did you feel most connected to today? Why?

Did you let go of anything today that was weighing on your heart?

Something I will do for self-care tomorrow is...

To be a better version of myself tomorrow, inshaAllah I will...

additional notes

DAY 27
ramadan

"Whoever believes in Allah and the Last Day,
should not hurt his neighbor and whoever
believes in Allah and the Last Day, should
serve his guest generously and whoever
believes in Allah and the Last Day, should
speak what is good or keep silent."

[Bukhari 6136]

Thoughts I choose to release as I begin today...

Take a moment to jot down everything on your mind—tasks, worries, grudges, anything at all. This quick exercise will help you begin your day with a clear heart & mind.

ramadan
DAY 27

my schedule

12 AM

1 AM

2 AM

3 AM

4 AM

5 AM

6 AM

7 AM

8 AM

9 AM

10 AM

11 AM

12 PM

1 PM

2 PM

3 PM

4 PM

5 PM

6 PM

7 PM

8 PM

9 PM

10 PM

11 PM

---

are you fasting today?

◯ YES   ◯ NO, I'M EXCUSED

DID YOU PAY YOUR FIDYAH? Y / N

suhoor ☀

iftar ☾

did you know...

Fasting can help reduce mood swings and irritability often associated with PMS by stabilizing blood sugar and promoting balanced hormone levels.

workout

◯ YES   ◯ NO

daily Quran:

	JUZZ	CHAPTER	VERSE
START:			
FINISH:			

good deeds:

◯ I GAVE IN CHARITY   ◯ I VISITED A SICK PERSON

◯ I HELPED SOMEONE IN NEED   ◯ I DID A SECRET GOOD DEED

◯ I FORGAVE SOMEONE   ◯ I SPOKE WITH MY PARENTS

◯ I FED A HUNGRY PERSON   ◯ I HOSTED IFTAR

prayers

◯ FAJR   ◯ ISHA

◯ DHUR   ◯ TARAWEEH

◯ ASR   ◯ TAHAJJUD

◯ MAGHRIB

adhkaar

◯ MORNING

◯ EVENING

additional notes

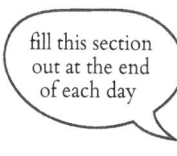

A moment for
Mindfulness

Now let's check-in with how you're feeling spiritually and emotionally...

I am feeling...

ANGRY   TIRED   SAD   HAPPY   EXCITED

I feel this way right now because...

Alhamdulillah for...

Have I taken a moment to pause, breathe, and reconnect with my intentions today?

Y / N

What spiritual lesson(s) did I learn today?

Which of Allah's names or attributes did you feel most connected to today? Why?

Did you let go of anything today that was weighing on your heart?

Something I will do for self-care tomorrow is...

To be a better version of myself tomorrow, inshaAllah I will...

additional notes

DAY 28
ramadan

"The best among you are those who have the
best manners and character."

[Bukhari 6029]

Thoughts I choose to release as I begin today...

Take a moment to jot down everything on your mind—tasks, worries, grudges, anything at all. This quick exercise will help you begin your day with a clear heart & mind.

ramadan
DAY 28

my schedule

12 AM

1 AM

2 AM

3 AM

4 AM

5 AM

6 AM

7 AM

8 AM

9 AM

10 AM

11 AM

12 PM

1 PM

2 PM

3 PM

4 PM

5 PM

6 PM

7 PM

8 PM

9 PM

10 PM

11 PM

are you fasting today?

○ YES   ○ NO, I'M EXCUSED

DID YOU PAY YOUR FIDYAH? Y / N

suhoor ☀

iftar ☾

did you know...

By balancing hormones, improving blood circulation, and reducing inflammation, fasting may help promote healthier, stronger hair growth and reduce hair thinning.

workout

○ YES   ○ NO

daily Quran:

	JUZZ	CHAPTER	VERSE
START:			
FINISH:			

good deeds:

○ I GAVE IN CHARITY   ○ I VISITED A SICK PERSON
○ I HELPED SOMEONE IN NEED   ○ I DID A SECRET GOOD DEED
○ I FORGAVE SOMEONE   ○ I SPOKE WITH MY PARENTS
○ I FED A HUNGRY PERSON   ○ I HOSTED IFTAR

prayers

○ FAJR   ○ ISHA
○ DHUR   ○ TARAWEEH
○ ASR   ○ TAHAJJUD
○ MAGHRIB

adhkaar

○ MORNING
○ EVENING

additional notes

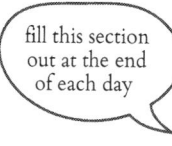

fill this section out at the end of each day

A moment for
Mindfulness

Now let's check-in with how you're feeling spiritually and emotionally...

I am feeling...

ANGRY   TIRED   SAD   HAPPY   EXCITED

I feel this way right now because...

Alhamdulillah for...

Have I taken a moment to pause, breathe, and reconnect with my intentions today?

Y / N

What spiritual lesson(s) did I learn today?

Which of Allah's names or attributes did you feel most connected to today? Why?

Did you let go of anything today that was weighing on your heart?

Something I will do for self-care tomorrow is...

To be a better version of myself tomorrow, inshaAllah I will...

additional notes

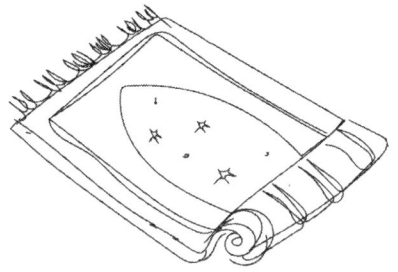

DAY 29
ramadan

"Indeed, Allah, is Hayy, Generous, when a
man raises his hands to Him, He feels too shy
to return them to him empty and rejected."

[Tirmidhi 3556]

Thoughts I choose to release as I begin today...

Take a moment to jot down everything on your mind—tasks, worries, grudges, anything at all. This quick exercise will help you begin your day with a clear heart & mind.

ramadan
DAY 29

my schedule

12 AM

1 AM

2 AM

3 AM

4 AM

5 AM

6 AM

7 AM

8 AM

9 AM

10 AM

11 AM

12 PM

1 PM

2 PM

3 PM

4 PM

5 PM

6 PM

7 PM

8 PM

9 PM

10 PM

11 PM

are you fasting today?

○ YES   ○ NO, I'M EXCUSED

DID YOU PAY YOUR FIDYAH? Y / N

suhoor ☼

iftar ☾

workout

○ YES   ○ NO

did you know...

Fasting gives your digestive system a break, allowing it to rest and repair. This can improve gut health, reduce bloating, and help regulate bowel movements.

daily Quran:

	JUZZ	CHAPTER	VERSE
START:			
FINISH:			

good deeds:

○ I GAVE IN CHARITY   ○ I VISITED A SICK PERSON

○ I HELPED SOMEONE IN NEED   ○ I DID A SECRET GOOD DEED

○ I FORGAVE SOMEONE   ○ I SPOKE WITH MY PARENTS

○ I FED A HUNGRY PERSON   ○ I HOSTED IFTAR

prayers

○ FAJR   ○ ISHA

○ DHUR   ○ TARAWEEH

○ ASR   ○ TAHAJJUD

○ MAGHRIB

adhkaar

○ MORNING

○ EVENING

additional notes

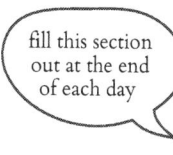

fill this section out at the end of each day

A moment for
Mindfulness

Now let's check-in with how you're feeling spiritually and emotionally...

I am feeling...

😠 😫 🙁 🙂 😆
ANGRY   TIRED   SAD   HAPPY   EXCITED

I feel this way right now because...

Alhamdulillah for...

Have I taken a moment to pause, breathe, and reconnect with my intentions today?

Y / N

What spiritual lesson(s) did I learn today?

Which of Allah's names or attributes did you feel most connected to today? Why?

Did you let go of anything today that was weighing on your heart?

Something I will do for self-care tomorrow is...

To be a better version of myself tomorrow, inshaAllah I will...

additional notes

DAY 30
ramadan

"Whoever fasts Ramadan then follows it with six
days of Shawwal, it is as if he fasted for a lifetime."

[Ibn Majah 1716]

Thoughts I choose to release as I begin today...

Take a moment to jot down everything on your mind—tasks, worries, grudges, anything at all. This quick exercise will help you begin your day with a clear heart & mind.

ramadan
DAY 30

my schedule

12 AM

1 AM

2 AM

3 AM

4 AM

5 AM

6 AM

7 AM

8 AM

9 AM

10 AM

11 AM

12 PM

1 PM

2 PM

3 PM

4 PM

5 PM

6 PM

7 PM

8 PM

9 PM

10 PM

11 PM

are you fasting today?

○ YES   ○ NO, I'M EXCUSED

DID YOU PAY YOUR FIDYAH? Y / N

suhoor ☀

iftar ☾

workout

○ YES   ○ NO

did you know...

While fasting, the production of saliva can decrease, which may lead to fewer oral bacteria and less plaque buildup, ultimately improving overall oral hygiene.

daily Quran:

	JUZZ	CHAPTER	VERSE
START:			
FINISH:			

good deeds:

○ I GAVE IN CHARITY   ○ I VISITED A SICK PERSON

○ I HELPED SOMEONE IN NEED   ○ I DID A SECRET GOOD DEED

○ I FORGAVE SOMEONE   ○ I SPOKE WITH MY PARENTS

○ I FED A HUNGRY PERSON   ○ I HOSTED IFTAR

prayers

○ FAJR   ○ ISHA

○ DHUR   ○ TARAWEEH

○ ASR   ○ TAHAJJUD

○ MAGHRIB

adhkaar

○ MORNING

○ EVENING

additional notes

fill this section out at the end of each day

A moment for
Mindfulness

Now let's check-in with how you're feeling spiritually and emotionally...

I am feeling...

ANGRY   TIRED   SAD   HAPPY EXCITED

I feel this way right now because...

Alhamdulillah for...

Have I taken a moment to pause, breathe, and reconnect with my intentions today?

Y / N

What spiritual lesson(s) did I learn today?

Which of Allah's names or attributes did you feel most connected to today? Why?

Did you let go of anything today that was weighing on your heart?

Something I will do for self-care tomorrow is...

To be a better version of myself tomorrow, inshaAllah I will...

additional notes

Farewell Ramadan

An opportunity to cherish &
reflect on lessons learned

As you reach the end of this Ramadan journal, take a moment to reflect on the profound journey you've undertaken over the past month.

Remember, the essence of Ramadan is about transformation. Just as the moon waxes and wanes, your journey of faith will have its phases. Commit to the good habits you have built during this month and carry them forward with you. Remember that the end of Ramadan should not signify the end of your spiritual journey—it is only the beginning. Ramadan has equipped you with tools for resilience and mindfulness; now, it is up to you to use them in your everyday life.

May Allah (SWT) accept your efforts, grant you strength in your endeavors, and shower you with His mercy and blessings. Remember, you are never alone on this journey. Each moment of prayer, reflection, and action you take adds to the collective spirit of our ummah. Continue to strive for excellence in your worship, and may your life reflect the beauty of Ramadan every day of the year.

Before you close this journal, take a moment to reflect over what Ramadan was like for you this year. Consider the challenges you faced, the growth you experienced, and the connections you made with others. This reflection will help you carry the blessings and lessons from Ramadan into the year ahead, allowing you to continue growing in faith and striving for a closer connection to your Lord.

What are some lessons from this Ramadan you want to keep with you?

What progress did you make this Ramadan?

Which new habits or practices will you continue after Ramadan?

How did your relationship with Allah (SWT) change in Ramadan?

What was hard for you this Ramadan?

What can you do to make it easier next year?

How can you keep the gratitude and peace
of Ramadan in your life year-round?

What was your most memorable moment this Ramadan?

Glossary

Adhkar: Remembrances and phrases recited to praise and worship Allah. (SWT)

Aishah: The wife of the Prophet Muhammad (SAW), known for her knowledge and contributions to Islam.

Akhirah: The afterlife.

Allah: The Arabic name for God—the Creator and Sustainer of the universe.

Al-Ghaffar: One of Allah's 99 names, meaning "The Forgiving."

Ameen: An Arabic term meaning "May it be so," said to affirm prayers.

Barakah: Blessings and divine favor from Allah (SWT).

Bayt ul-'Izzah: The "House of Honor"—a heavenly place where the Quran was revealed in its entirety before being sent to the Prophet Muhammad (SAW).

Da'wah: The act of inviting others to Islam.

Deen: Religion, particularly referring to Islam.

Dua': Supplication or prayer made directly to Allah (SWT).

Eid Mubarak: A greeting meaning "Blessed Eid," exchanged during the two Eid celebrations.

Eid ul-Adha: The festival of sacrifice, commemorating Prophet Ibrahim's (PBUH) willingness to sacrifice his son.

Eid ul-Fitr: The Islamic celebration marking the end of Ramadan.

Fidyah: Compensation given for missed fasts due to valid reasons.

Five Daily Prayers: The obligatory prayers: *Fajr* (dawn), *Dhuhr* (midday), *Asr* (afternoon), *Maghrib* (sunset), *Isha* (night).

Hadith: Recorded sayings, actions, and approvals of the Prophet Muhammad (SAW).

Hadith Qudsi: Sacred sayings of Allah (SWT) conveyed through the Prophet (SAW) but not part of the Quran.

Hasanaat: Good deeds rewarded by Allah (SWT).

Imam al-Shafi'i: A prominent Islamic jurist and founder of one of the four major Sunni schools of thought.

Imam Ibn Rajab al-Hanbali: An Islamic scholar known for his works on hadith and spirituality.

Insha'Allah: A phrase meaning "If Allah wills," used to express hope for future events.

Istighfaar: Seeking forgiveness from Allah (SWT).

Jannah: Paradise—the eternal home of reward for the righteous in the afterlife.

Jannatul Firdaws: The highest level of Paradise, reserved for the most pious believers.

Jibreel: The Angel Gabriel, who conveyed Allah's (SWT) revelations to the prophets.

Khawaarij: A sect that emerged after the Prophet Muhammad's (SAW) time, known for their extreme and misguided interpretations of Islam.

Khushoo': A state of humility and concentration in worship.

Lawhul Mahfuz: The "Preserved Tablet," where all divine decrees are written.

Laylatul Qadr: The "Night of Decree"—a blessed night in Ramadan when the Quran was first revealed.

Limiting Beliefs: Thoughts or assumptions that hinder personal growth or success.

Masjid: A mosque—the place of worship for Muslims.

Mushrikeen: Those who associate partners with Allah (SWT) in worship.

Mus'haf: The physical, written copy of the Quran.

Mustahabb: Actions that are recommended in Islam but not obligatory.

Nawafil: Voluntary prayers or acts of worship beyond the obligatory.

PBUH: An abbreviation for "Peace Be Upon Him," a phrase of respect traditionally said by Muslims after mentioning the name of a prophet.

Prophet Adam: The first human and prophet in Islam.

Prophet Muhammad: The final prophet in Islam, who received the Quran and guided humanity to the path of righteousness.

Prophet Zakariyyah: A prophet in Islam known for his devotion and patience.

Qiblah: The direction Muslims face during prayer, towards the Kabah in Makkah.

Quran: The holy book of Islam, revealed to the Prophet Muhammad (SAW) over 23 years.

RA: Abbreviation for *Radi Allahu Anhu/Anha/Anhum*, meaning "May Allah be pleased with him/her/them," used for companions of the Prophet (SAW).

Rabb: Lord or Sustainer, referring to Allah (SWT).

Ramadan: The ninth month of the Islamic calendar, observed with fasting from dawn to sunset as an act of worship.

Ramadan Mubarak: A greeting meaning "Blessed Ramadan," often exchanged at the start of the holy month.

Rakah: A unit of prayer in salah.

Rasulullah: "Messenger of Allah," referring to the Prophet Muhammad (SAW).

Sadaqah: Voluntary charity given to help those in need.

SAW: Acronym for *Sallallahu Alayhi wa Sallam*, meaning "Peace and blessings be upon him," used after mentioning the Prophet Muhammad (SAW).

Sahaaba: The companions of the Prophet Muhammad (SAW) who supported him and spread Islam.

Salawat: Prayers for blessings upon the Prophet Muhammad (SAW).

Salaf: The early generations of Muslims, including the Prophet's (SAW) companions, their successors, and the following generation.

Salah: The five daily prayers that are obligatory for Muslims.

Sunnah: The practices and teachings of the Prophet Muhammad (SAW).

Suhoor: The pre-dawn meal before fasting begins during Ramadan.

Surah: A chapter of the Quran.

SWT: Abbreviation for *Subhanahu wa Ta'ala*, meaning "Glorified and Exalted is He," used to show reverence for Allah (SWT).

Taqwa: Consciousness and reverence of Allah (SWT), leading to righteous living.

Takbeer: The phrase "Allahu Akbar," meaning "Allah is the Greatest."

Tahajjud: Voluntary night prayer performed in the later part of the night.

Taharah: Ritual purity in Islam.

Talbinah: Talbinah is a traditional dish made from barley flour, milk, and honey, recommended by the Prophet Muhammad (SAW) for its healing benefits, particularly for emotional well-being. It was prescribed as a comforting food for those experiencing grief or sadness, highlighting its soothing qualities and potential mental health benefits, supported by its nutritional richness.

<u>Taraweeh:</u> Special prayers performed during Ramadan nights.

<u>Tawheed:</u> The oneness and uniqueness of Allah (SWT) in worship and attributes.

About the Author

Kashmir Maryam is a therapist and author. She is celebrated for her unique insights on mindfulness, spirituality, and personal growth. Her books focus on mental health and emotional well-being, integrating Islamic guidance from the Quran and Sunnah.

Kashmir is the Founding Director of the *Heal Therapy Clinic*, an organization that provides mental health support to the Muslim community. You can stay connected with Kashmir and her latest work on social media here:

@kashmirmaryam
@healtherapyclinic

Dear Reader, if you're struggling with personal challenges, relationship issues, or just need space to process and grow, our team of Muslim therapists is here to walk alongside you.

Scan the QR code to take the first step toward getting the support you need:

www.healtherapy.org

About the Publisher

Mindful Muslim Press is a publishing house dedicated to enhancing the mental health and mindfulness of Muslims world-wide. Our mission is to empower readers with tools for personal growth, healing, and self-awareness, rooted in Islamic values.

> *Bulk copies of this book are available for study circles, schools, community programs, and bookstores. To place a wholesale order, please contact the distributor through the website listed below.*

mindfulmuslimpress.org

Printed in Dunstable, United Kingdom